My BLACK & DECKER TOASTER OVEN

Easy Meal Cookbook

101 Surprisingly Delicious Recipes For Your T01303SB Countertop Oven

By

Tara Adams

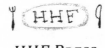

HHF Press
San Francisco

Legal Notice

The information contained in this book is for entertainment purposes only. The content represents the opinion of the author and is based on the author's personal experience and observations. The author does not assume any liability whatsoever for the use of or inability to use any or all information contained in this book, and accepts no responsibility for any loss or damages of any kind that may be incurred by the reader as a result of actions arising from the use of information in this book. Use this information at your own risk.

The author reserves the right to make any changes he or she deems necessary to future versions of the publication to ensure its accuracy.

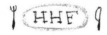

ISBN-13: 978-1540503930
ISBN-10: 1540503933

Published in the United States of America
by Healthy Happy Foodie Press.

www.HHFpress.com

DO YOU LIKE FREE BOOKS?

Every month we release a new book, and we offer it to our current readers first...absolutely free! This helps us get early feedback before launching a book, and lets you stock your shelf full of interesting and valuable books for free!

Some recent titles include:

- The Complete Vegetable Spiralizer Cookbook
- My Lodge Cast Iron Skillet Cookbook
- 101 The New Crepes Cookbook

To receive this month's free book, just go to

http://www.healthyhappyfoodie.org/ee1-freebooks

Table Of Contents

Dinner Recipes

1

Why You Need This Book!

It is a fair question to ask and I have some answers for you. This isn't just some dry text, it is filled with information and personality. It doesn't read like a dry owner's manual but more like a spunky cookbook that doesn't only offer recipes, but solid advice to use your toaster oven like a true professional. Here are a few of the many reasons why you need this book.

It's The Only Book Written Just for The Black and Decker Toaster Oven

Toaster ovens have been around for a long time so this is not the first toaster oven book ever written; it is however the first ever written specifically for this machine. Being the only toaster oven book written solely about the Black and Decker Toaster oven, means it's filled with some of the ideas of the other books, a whole lot of new information, and plenty of information which is specific to this oven. It is written from the perspective of someone who has used—and loved—this toaster oven. You will find all kinds of hints and tips that will allow you to use your Black and

Decker, or any toaster oven to its maximum capacity, and quickly make it your favorite kitchen appliance.

Learn How to Cook Delicious Meals and Snacks...Without a Traditional Oven!

That's right, with one machine you will become the talk of the next get together. It is not just parties that you will become a hero, your own family will also start taking notice. There is a difference between just throwing some food in a toaster oven and unlocking what it means to be a true toaster over chef. This book will teach you the ideas you need and how to implement them in order to get delicious and perfectly cooked foods every time you use your Black and Decker. To be clear, we are not just talking pizza and grilled cheese, you are going to learn how to cook fantastic full meals, sensational snacks, and desirable deserts all with a single machine.

Learn Surprising Pro Tips and Tricks to Turn your Toaster Oven into a Gourmet-quality Kitchen!

This isn't going to read like some dry copy straight from the manufacturer and it is definitely not from the point of view of someone who hasn't even used a toaster oven. You are going to learn how to use your toaster oven in traditional ways that transform ordinary foods into extraordinary foods. You will also learn how to use your toaster oven in unconventional ways to make the most of a single appliance.

The book is filled with great ideas which are simple to implement, but make a huge difference in your kitchen. While the book is fun, it is also practical, you will learn just as many important tips about things like care and storage of your device as you will about all of the fun stuff. By the time you are done reading it you will want to head to the kitchen right away and start cooking anything and everything you can.

Over 100 Mouthwatering Recipes Just for Your Toaster Oven

This book isn't just 100 different ways to cook bread. It isn't even a pizza recipe book. It is a real live cookbook filled with over 100 delicious recipes designed to fulfill every need from that extra side with dinner to the entire meal. These recipes are not just bland everyday items either; you will be privy to some of the best toaster oven recipes to ever be created. The only problem you will have with these recipes is figuring out which one you want to try first.

2

Why Choose Black and Decker?

Exclusive Even Toast Technology

Even Toast technology is basically a fancy way of saying that this machine was built with purpose to cook as evenly as possible across your food no matter what you are cooking. This is actually a big deal because one of the biggest downsides to toaster ovens is their inability to maintain heat which is why it is not advised to cook some foods in a toaster oven. Even Toast technology makes the Black and Decker better, more efficient, and even safer than other more expensive models.

High Quality at a Fraction of the Price

When I went shopping for a toaster oven, I could not believe how expensive some of them were; and for what? They all pretty much do the same thing; so why do you need to pay in the hundreds when you could get the perfect toaster oven for under $50? The machine is small, but sturdy and when you put your hands on it you can tell that it is made out of quality materials. The Even Toast technology is only one of the reasons why this machine is such high quality. They use stainless steel which is a must in the kitchen and specifically design the racks to accommodate a variety of meals.

Every inch of this machine is hand crafted and perfectly designed to fit into not just your kitchen, but also your life. The most important thing to remember here is that this is a Black and Decker product, which means it has over 100 years of quality behind it. Honestly, you would be hard pressed to find a better toaster oven at this size, and there is no way you would find one of its quality at its price point.

Smaller Footprint, Sleek Design

Other than the price, one of the biggest benefits to the Black and Decker toaster oven is its small footprint. Having to take your toaster oven out and put it away every time you want to use it is not only a hassle, but it takes up valuable cupboard space. Having a small footprint means that you can leave it out on the counter and it won't interfere with your counter space or your cupboard space. The only downside to that is having to look at toaster oven every time you walk into the kitchen, but Black and Decker has you covered there too.

This toaster oven isn't just small; it has a well thought out design which makes it not so bad to look at. The use of black molded parts and a stainless steel exterior make it a perfect addition to many modern kitchens and the curved box design offers timeless shape with contemporary elements. In other words, it will look more like a part of your kitchen than a standard toaster does.

Safer Than Other Toaster Ovens, and Uses Less Energy

There are so many reasons why this oven is a safer alternative to other ovens. For one, the smaller size means less hot surface area to burn anything that comes around it. The fact that it uses a 3 pronged power cord helps to avoid electrical mishaps and the fact this automatically shuts off when the timer is done means you don't need to worry about accidently leaving it on. The crumb tray is easy to slide out which means you won't leave excess crumbs in your machine to start burning and the large, clear window means that you will always be able to see if your food is overcooking. It's not just safety that the Black and Decker oven excels at, it also uses a lot less energy than those other brands.

The fact that it is so small means that it is automatically going to use less energy than other models. Not only does it need less electricity, but it heats up faster and keeps its heat longer all of which make for less energy consumption. The fact that it automatically shuts off when the timer goes off is not just great for safety, but also means that only the necessary amount of energy will be used every time. For both safety and energy savings, remember to unplug your toaster oven when it is not being used.

Black and Decker Known for Durable and Long Lasting Products

Yeah, it's built well; but how well built? Black and Decker is well known for how durable and long lasting their products are which is probably why they have been in business for over 100 years. While random anomalies are a fact of life, for the most part Black and Decker toaster oven users have nothing but good things to say about their experience. Even someone who uses this oven once or more every day will probably not have to replace it for years. If for some reason there is a problem with the machine it is warrantied for two years after the original purchase date. Two years may not seem that spectacular, but that is a nice length of time for a budget friendly small appliance.

3

What Your Toaster Oven Can Do

Cook Full Meals

There is an idea held by many that since it has the word "toast" in the name that all a toaster oven can do is cook bread. Of course it is great for making anything from regular toast to some pretty spectacular cooked breads, but that is only the beginning.

BREAKFAST

It's funny to start with breakfast, because, of course, toast. But toast is only one part of a balanced breakfast. You can cook an entire breakfast in a toaster oven including eggs, bacon, and even hash browns; just keep the orange juice away from the toaster.

LUNCH

Lunch is one of my favorite times to use the toaster oven, because it is perfect to whip together a hot lunch. It makes a great sandwich melts and can even reheat last night's left overs to the perfect temperature. It's not just the main meal that the toaster oven is good at, it can cook plenty of lunch-sized sides like French fries, baked veggies, and even homemade potato chips.

DINNER

Again, this machine is perfect for cooking leftovers, but there is so much more that it can do. A machine of this size does not lend itself to cooking thick meats, but it can cook some meats for dinnertime meals. Just like for lunch you can cook a whole host of sides that are perfect for dinner. It can even cook some delicious desserts to finish your nightly meal.

SNACKS

It's not just good for the main meals either, the Black and Decker toaster oven is great for cooking hundreds of between meal snacks.

Make Delicious Sides, including Fries and Vegetables

It is truly a one-stop shop for a healthier way to cook everything from the main dish to a number of sides. You can cook almost any side imaginable with this machine including fries, homemade potato chips, full potatoes, a number of baked vegetables, biscuits, soups, and even stuffing. At the very least it offers an extra oven to cook your sides in while you are cooking the main meal in a traditional oven.

Toast, Cook, Broil, and Defrost Almost as Well as Any Oven

Toast

Obviously this machine was made for toasting and in many ways does it better than a traditional toaster. It toasts the perfect bread better than a standard oven and does it in a fraction of the time. It also allows you to toast thicker breads that you couldn't toast in a traditional toaster like thick garlic bread or hoagie rolls for sandwiches.

Cook

Also known as baking when it comes to an oven, the Black and Decker can do almost anything that a traditional oven can do and usually in half the time. Of course the partition sizes are going to be a lot smaller in a toaster oven. There are a few exceptions here but thanks to advances in technology you can cook most of your favorites using less energy and in half the time.

Broil

If they weren't called toaster ovens they would be called broiling ovens. The whole point behind broiling is to thoroughly cook thin foods at high temperatures for short periods of time. Nothing does this better than a toaster oven and few toaster ovens do it better than the Black and Decker.

Defrost

One function of the toaster oven that often goes overlooked is its ability to defrost foods. I love using my toaster oven to defrost because it defrosts more evenly than the microwave. It usually takes the same time, sometimes a bit longer, but the wait is worth it for perfectly defrosted food ready to cook. The glass window also allows you to see when the food is perfectly defrosted and remove your foods before they start to cook.

Make Arts and Crafts!

This is an idea that will surprise many people, but a toaster oven is actually an ideal machine for arts and crafts. It can be used in any number of ways and is fairly kid friendly with adult supervision. There are a ton of ways that you can use your toaster oven for crafts, and it can even be a way to make a little extra cash on the side by selling arts and jewelry. We will touch on this a little more later in the book with some arts and crafts ideas.

4

How to Use your Toaster Oven

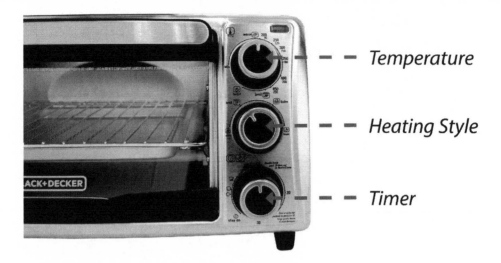

The Knobs

Honestly, the knobs on this oven can be confusing at first glance. Here's the skinny:

- Top knob—use this to control temperature.
- Middle knob—used for cooking function (i.e. warm, roast, bake). This adjusts the toaster's heating style.
- Last knob—basically used as a timer or as a "darkness" setting for your toast.

Quick Start:

1. Make sure that your toaster oven is clean and everything is in its proper place, if not, clean it with the cleaning instructions I have provided in the next segment.

2. Find a clean, level, heat resistant, open area to place your oven so there won't be any worry about heating damage. (If your oven remains on the counter at all times skip this step.)

3. Plug the machine into the wall.

4. Set the temperature selection and the cooking mode using the knobs.

5. Place your food onto the rack using an oven safe container or the cooking instructions provided with the food.

6. When your food is done cooking open the door and let any built up heat escape.

7. Making sure to use heat resistant mitts, pull the rack out and remove your food.

8. Place the food on a heat resistant surface to cool.

9. Unplug the machine to avoid electrical problems and save energy.

How to Clean

- Start by making sure that your toaster oven is unplugged.

- Remove the crumb tray and shake out the crumbs before wiping it clean with a damp towel. Set it aside to let it dry. If there are a lot of stuck on crumbs there is no harm in rinsing the crumb tray in the sink, just be sure that it is completely dry before putting it back in the oven.

- Fill a bowl with warm soapy water and use a towel or soft sponge to wipe the inside of the oven and the elements. Use another damp (just water) towel to wipe the same surfaces to remove any soap residue. Allow to dry completely before plugging your machine back in.

- The window is an important part of your toaster oven and it is important to keep it clean and streak free without the risk of harsh chemicals being used. The best way to accomplish this is to use cleaning vinegar on the in and outside of the glass it cleans great, is all-natural, and leaves a streak free shine.

- For tough baked on grease and grime, first pour baking soda on the window and then vinegar. The chemical reaction is usually good to break up and lift anything that is stuck on the window.

- If there is some really tough stuff baked on to the window or anywhere in the oven use a razor blade to scrape off what you can before trying steps 5 and 4.

- The outside of the machine is usually easily cleaned with warm soapy water, but if needed you can use a degreasing agent since food will most likely not touch these surfaces. You may want to wipe it down with a damp cloth afterwards to prevent a chemical smell the next time you warm up your oven.

How to Keep Safe While Using Your Toaster Oven

The most important safety tip of all is to be sure to keep bodies and items away from the oven when it is on. These ovens can get super-heated and cause serious injuries, start fires, and ruin valuables if left unchecked.

Always read your owner's manual before using; there could be instructions in there that you may not have thought of and it is always better to be safe than sorry.

Pick a heat resistant spot that is preferably in a low traffic area and away from anything highly flammable like paper towels or curtains. Also make sure that you give yourself a foot or two of space underneath any cabinets to avoid warping or even burning your cabinets from the heat of the oven.

Never let children use the toaster oven unattended; though they are usually safer than a traditional oven, they still get pretty hot and can cause injury.

Always use safety utensils (oven mitts for example) when removing hot food from the oven.

Never use any food-serving dish that is not specifically labeled for high heats.

Make a habit out of turning the oven off right away. It will save energy and decrease chances of fire and injury.

Be careful when reheating liquids. There is always a possibility of superheating liquids when you are warming them up or even defrosting them from a frozen state. Be extremely careful when removing liquids from the oven as they could spill and cause injury to any uncovered areas.

5

How to Use Your Toaster Oven Like an Expert

If you are buying a toaster oven just for toast, then you are buying it for all of the wrong reasons. This machine is capable of so much more and this chapter will teach you how to unlock its hidden potential.

How to Defrost and Melt Foods

Toaster ovens are not often thought of as a way to quickly defrost foods, but they are one of the best at it. The Black and Decker does not have a defrost setting, but it does have a warm setting which is pretty much the same thing. If you are defrosting something like bread you can put it on a rack, but if you are defrosting something a little juicer like a steak, be sure to put in a pan deep enough to catch any of the blood and juices that will be released; this makes clean up much easier.

The same method can be used to perfectly melt cheese over anything, which is especially awesome when you are making sandwich melts. There is no exact science to defrosting or melting so you kind of have to watch the food and remove it before it starts to cook or over-cook depending on what you are using it for. Luckily this toaster oven has a decently sized window so you will easily be able to see the status of your food.

Understanding Even Toast Technology

What exactly is Even Toast Technology? The toaster is designed specifically to optimize the distribution of heat more evenly across foods. The heating coils are placed perfectly to regulate heat up to 30 percent more evenly than competitors which leads to more even cooking. It is not just a benefit for toasting, but other cooking methods like defrosting and broiling as well. It seems like a simple idea, but it makes this toaster oven more efficient than those models that cost a few hundred dollars.

\

Understand The Difference Between Warm, Broil, Bake, and Roast

To become a master toaster oven chef, you must really understand what each setting means and how to best use them.

WARM

We already touched on this a little, but the warm setting has many purposes. It can be used to defrost frozen foods, perfectly melt cheese over foods, and most importantly, to warm up leftovers. Instead of zapping your leftovers with microwaves and potentially over cooking it, just put it in the toaster oven for a few minutes. It may take a few more minutes than a microwave, but your food will come out at the perfect temperature and ready to eat.

BROIL

We touched on broiling earlier, but it is good to revisit it because many inexperienced cooks really don't understand how broiling works. Traditional cooking on a stovetop or in an oven—even in a microwave—works by cooking the food from the outside in which usually takes longer periods of time at lower temperatures. Broiling basically flash cooks the entire food by exposing it to super high heat directly above, which makes for a quick way to cook many foods, especially thin cuts of meat. Broiling however doesn't work for every food and takes a little practice to get right. Again the small space and ability to reach over 450 degrees quickly make toaster ovens perfect for broiling.

BAKE

It is an oven after all. There is so much that you can do with a toaster oven that it is easy to forget that it can bake all of your favorite treats and snacks just like a regular oven only in smaller batches. This is great for someone who loves to bake, but doesn't need to bake for a whole family. It also wastes less energy and can bake great meals for one like potpies.

ROAST

Roasting is the act of cooking foods using dry heat that surrounds the food. People often roast meats, vegetables, and nuts, and some people swear that roasting is the best way to bring out the flavor in foods.

Use for Arts and Crafts

SHRINK ART

Shrink art has been a popular kid's craft since it was invented in 1973. Shrink art is made by creating shapes and images out of large sheets of polystyrene plastic and coloring them with any number of coloring material. Then you just pop them in the toaster oven and they maintain their shape and color, but shrink and harden. It is a great craft for kids, but also awesome for adults looking to make jewelry.

POP ART BOARDS

These fun little boards are a delight for kids. They are flat boards and kids get to color them just like they would any regular coloring page. The only difference is that when placed in the toaster oven the page pops like popcorn and you get an amazing textured art piece.

MAKE CRAYONS

Well, maybe not so much make crayons, as re-use them. If you have a lot of broken crayons lying around you can break them up into oven safe molds and melt them down. Simply pull them out and let them cool back down and solidify. You get some cool looking tie dyed crayons that color a rainbow and are shaped however you want them to be.

MAKE CRAZY CUP ART

Some adventurous artists use their toaster oven to soften plastic cups in order to mold them into any shape they want, or even join multiple shapes together. Just like shrink art, they can be colored using almost any medium and the cups usually hold the color. This can lead to some pretty awesome works of art, especially for someone with a creative mind.

PONY BEAD SUN CATCHERS

This one is super simple and can create some really cool looking artwork that the kids will love. Simply use a muffin tin or small baking tin to make a design using translucent pony beads. Pop them in the oven at 400 degrees for around 25 minutes, then pull them out and let them cool. The finished product is a beautiful translucent sun catcher, just drill a hole and add a suction cup hook. This craft can produce a strong odor of plastic melting so you may want to do it outside, luckily a toaster oven is easily portable.

I am sure there a plenty of other examples of arts and crafts that can be done with your toaster oven, but you bought a recipe book, not a craft book; so I will leave it at that.

6

Pro Tips

Do Not Use Aluminum Foil – Other Options!

Most people will tell you that this is a toaster oven, not a microwave, but there are still some risks when it comes to using aluminum foil in a toaster oven. Even though it is metal it can still catch on fire—which spells disaster—and might even throw off the thermostat in the machine. Some people even think that there are health risks involved with aluminum foil. Here are a few options that you could use instead of aluminum foil:

- Use a pan with a glass lid. Finding one small enough for this appliance may be a bit of a challenge, but it is the best option. This allows the heat to permeate through the pan for even cooking without focusing too much heat on the food.

- Silicone is a material that is growing in popularity for cooking. I personally own a set of silicone baking pans because they are easy to store, hold their shape, and stand up to high heats. They are also non-stick which is really nice because they are easy to clean and food pops right out of them.

- Parchment paper is another material that would work in some situations, but the risks are nearly the same so it is a good idea to use parchment paper only as a pan liner.

- Skip the foil for potatoes. Maybe foil is needed for grilling or cooking in fire, but it is not actually needed for baking. Simply placing the potatoes on a pan and sliding them in the oven is enough to bake a great potato.

- If you are looking to cook/grill/roast vegetables look into a grill basket. Most are small enough to slide into a toaster oven, and they are a perfect way to cook veggies, and other small loose foods, while keeping them together in one place.

- Some people who have a sensitivity to aluminum foil choose to use banana leaves instead. I don't personally have any experience with them, but people swear by them and it seems like a really cool idea.

If you absolutely must use aluminum foil make sure to use a clean sheet every time, this will reduce some of the risks.

What to Look for in the See Through Window

The see through window in the toaster oven is definitely one of the toaster oven's best qualities, it is especially nice with this particular toaster oven because of its size compared to the rest of the machine. Any cook knows that there are always anomalies in cooking and just because you put something in at the right temperature for the correct amount of time doesn't always mean that it is going to cook perfectly. The best part about the window is it allows you to check on your food without having to open the oven door and let out precious cooking heat.

Use your window to make sure that your food is not touching the sides or the heating elements of the oven. Watch for overcooking, the last thing you want is to burn your food when you are in a hurry. Having the window is awesome because you can check in whenever you want to make sure that the food is cooking evenly and not burning. The same goes for defrosting, when you are defrosting foods you want to make sure that they are defrosting and not actually cooking as this could lead to uneven when you actually start cooking the food.

How to Gauge the Right Sized Food

If your oven is 11 inches wide you know that you should not put a 12-inch pizza in it, but you may not realize that you shouldn't put an 11-inch pizza in it either. When food touches the sides and heating coils of a toaster oven it causes all sorts of problems so it is important to know how to gauge the size of food that you are putting in your oven. There should always be room for air to move around the food since this is how the oven cooks; if you have too many slices of bread pressed up against each other, for example, the insides of the crusts will not cook and you will end up with half of your toast being soft.

Some toaster ovens are designed to cook thick meats, but not this particular model. There are still a lot of meats that you can cook in here like bacon, thin cut steaks and pork chops, and even small portions of ribs. Items like thick cuts, large portions of chicken, or anything big enough to get close to the sides and heating elements are not advised.

What's The Maximum Amount of Food You Can Put Inside?

Again, as long as there is enough airflow around the food and it is not touching the sides or the heating elements you should be good. The best rule to gauge the right amount food is portions of two or less. If you are cooking a single or a double portion of something you should be alright. Not only does this help to cook food faster and better, but it has the added benefit of portion control. Keep in mind that some foods, like bread, will grow a little while cooking so plan ahead for this expansion.

How to Store Leftover Food

Even though cooking in the toaster oven usually produces less food, there is always a chance for leftovers. In some cases, you may be purposefully cooking batches of food to eat or serve at a later date. Here are a few great ways to store food to ensure its freshness later on:

TOAST

Who stores toast; right? It is actually quite convenient for food preparation to have toast at your disposal, especially if you are making breakfast or sandwiches somewhere away from your kitchen. Let the toast cool completely, then wrap it in paper followed by tin foil. This should keep most of the crispness, then when you are ready you can warm it up if you have the option and serve.

PIZZA

Start by allowing your pizza to cool completely, excess heat causes condensation that will leave your pizza crust soggy. Line a plate or large glass container with paper towels, place your pizza on the towels and then cover the top again with paper towels. Add the lid or cover the plate with plastic wrap and store in the fridge.

MEAT AND POTATOES

If you are cooking a meal to eat later or are just storing leftovers, there is a proper way to store them to improve texture and taste in the future. First, you want to let them cool completely; this prevent condensation that builds up and makes your food soggy, or even wet to the touch. Next, put the food in an airtight glass container, glass works better than plastic at keeping air out. Lastly you want to refrigerate it as quickly as you can after it has cooled, this prevents bacteria from getting in and helps the food to maintain its taste and texture.

ROASTED NUTS

Nuts can be particularly hard to store because they can end up going rancid if you don't store them properly. If you are cooking large batches of nuts you are going to want to store them in an airtight container like a freezer bag or glass container with an airtight lid. They are also sensitive to heat and light so if you plan on eating them soon you should store them in a cool, dark place. If you don't have immediate plans to eat them, nuts can be stored in the freezer for up to 2 years. When you are ready to eat them, or use them to bake, simply pull them out and let them air defrost.

OTHER PANTRY ITEMS

Everything else that you cook can be stored in a similar fashion to nuts. Cooked (dried) Herbs, for example, should be stored in an airtight glass container and placed in a cool dark place.

How to Reheat Leftover Food

This one can get a little tricky, so it is good to touch on. Always, ALWAYS, <u>use the warm setting</u>! Toaster ovens heat pretty fast so your food will reheat fast even on the warm setting. Trying to speed up the process by putting it on a higher setting is only going to burn your food and cause a potential fire.

Place your food on an oven safe dish, or in a shallow pan and slide it into the oven. Cover the dish with something to protect the food from being burned. A glass storage container with a glass lid is the best way to expedite the process by taking it straight from the fridge and placing it straight into the oven. Some people use foil to cover their food, but as stated before, I don't recommend it. Set your toaster oven to warm, food differs so you can play around with the time, or just watch through the window and remove it when the food looks like it has been brought back to life.

This is the best way to reheat pizza to eat because it will usually crisp the crust at least a little bit instead of giving you the droopy crust that a microwave causes. I rarely cover my pizza so both the cheese and the crust get maximum exposure to the heating elements.

I also like to reheat pancakes in the toaster oven. You can cook a bunch on Monday and store them in the fridge. Put them in a shallow pan and pop them in the oven for a few minutes, they fluff up nicely and are perfectly warmed for serving.

If you are reheating grains (rice, pasta, etc.) sprinkle a teaspoon of water over them before reheating. It helps to keep them from drying out or baking.

7

Breakfast Recipes

Baked Apple Breakfast Oats

Servings: 1 | Prep Time: 15 Minutes | Cook Time: 15 Minutes

This recipe is super simple, but so delicious. With only a few ingredients it is a great way to throw together a quick breakfast in a hurry.

Ingredients:

1/3 cup vanilla greek yogurt

1/3 cup rolled oats

1 apple

1 tablespoon peanut butter

Directions:

1. Preheat your Black and Decker toaster oven to 400 degrees and set it on the warm setting.
2. Cut your apples into chunks approximately 1/2-inch-thick.
3. Place apples on an oven safe dish with some space between each chunk and sprinkle with cinnamon.
4. Bake in the oven for 12 minutes.
5. Combine yogurt and oats in a bowl.
6. Remove the apples from the oven and combine with the yogurt.
7. Top with peanut butter and you have a delicious and high protein breakfast.

Nutritional Info: Calories: 350, Sodium: 134 mg, Dietary Fiber: 8.1 g, Total Fat: 11.2 g, Total Carbs: 52.5 g, Protein: 12.7 g.

Buttery Chocolate Toast

Servings: 1 | Prep Time: 5 Minutes | Cook Time: 5 Minutes

It may be simple, but that doesn't stop it from being delicious. Make this magnificent take on toast in only a few minutes.

Ingredients:

Whole wheat bread slices

Coconut oil

Pure maple syrup

Cacao powder

Directions:

1. Start by toasting the bread in your toaster oven.

2. Spread the coconut oil over the toast.

3. Drizzle maple syrup in lines over the toast.

4. Sprinkle cacao powder and serve.

Nutritional Info: Calories: 101, Sodium: 133 mg, Dietary Fiber: 2.4 g, Total Fat: 3.5 g, Total Carbs: 14.8 g, Protein: 4.0 g.

Cheesy Baked Egg Toast

Servings: 4 | Prep Time: 10 Minutes | Cook Time: 10 Minutes

Just the name sounds delicious, but just wait until you see the finished product. This is one of my favorite breakfast meals, hands down.

Ingredients:

4 slices of wheat bread

4 eggs

1 cup shredded cheese

2 tablespoons softened butter

Directions:

1. Start by preheating your toaster oven to 350 degrees.

2. Place your bread on a greased baking sheet.

3. Use a teaspoon to push a square into the bread creating a little bed for the egg.

4. Sprinkle salt and pepper over the bread.

5. Break one egg into each square. Spread butter over each edge of the bread.

6. Sprinkle 1/4 cup cheese over buttered area.

7. Bake for 10 minutes or until the egg is solid and the cheese is golden brown.

Nutritional Info: Calories: 297, Sodium: 410 mg, Dietary Fiber: 1.9 g, Total Fat: 20.4 g, Total Carbs: 12.3 g, Protein: 16.3 g.

Ham and Cheese Bagel Sandwiches

Servings: 2 | Prep Time: 5 Minutes | Cook Time: 5 Minutes

These sandwiches are perfect meal to cook fast and take on the go. It doesn't hurt that they taste as spectacular as they look.

Ingredients:

2 bagels

4 teaspoons honey mustard

4 slices cooked honey ham

4 slices Swiss cheese

Directions:

1. Start by preheating your toaster oven to 400 degrees.

2. Spread honey mustard on each half of the bagel.

3. Add ham and cheese and close the bagel.

4. Bake the sandwich until the cheese is fully melted, it should take about 5 minutes.

Nutritional Info: Calories: 588, Sodium: 1450 mg, Dietary Fiber: 2.3 g, Total Fat: 20.1 g, Total Carbs: 62.9 g, Protein: 38.4 g.

Peanut Butter and Jelly Banana Boats

Servings: 1 | Prep Time: 5 Minutes | Cook Time: 15 Minutes

This recipe is great for a fun breakfast packed with everything you need to start the day or a mid-day snack to keep the energy up.

Ingredients:

1 banana

1/4 cup peanut butter

1/4 cup jelly

1 tablespoon granola

Directions:

1.   Start by preheating your toaster oven to 350 degrees.
2.   Slice the banana lengthwise and separate slightly.
3.   Spread peanut butter and jelly in the gap.
4.   Sprinkle granola over the entire banana.
5.   Bake for 15 minutes.

Nutritional Info: Calories: 724, Sodium: 327 mg, Dietary Fiber: 9.2 g, Total Fat: 36.6 g, Total Carbs: 102.9 g, Protein: 20.0 g.

Peanut Butter Cookies

Servings: 1 | Prep Time: 10 Minutes | Cook Time: 10 Minutes

This recipe is awesome because it has all the deliciousness of traditional peanut butter cookies, but in a single serving batch.

Ingredients:

2 tablespoon flour

1 1/2 tablespoons peanut butter

1/16 teaspoon baking soda

Pinch of salt

1/4 teaspoon pure vanilla extract

1 1/2 tablespoons maple syrup

1 teaspoon applesauce

Directions:

1. Start by pre-heating the toaster oven to 350 degrees.
2. Mix all of the dry ingredients together in one bowl.
3. Mix in peanut butter, then the rest of the ingredients.
4. Spray a small pan and drop cookies onto pan, then flatten.
5. Bake for 10 minutes.

Nutritional Info: Calories: 281, Sodium: 348 mg, Dietary Fiber: 1.9 g, Total Fat: 12.3 g, Total Carbs: 37.5 g, Protein: 7.6 g.

Poached Eggs with Avocado and Spinach

Servings: 1 | Prep Time: 7 Minutes | Cook Time: 10 Minutes

Even the name is mouth-watering, this recipe is simple to cook and doesn't have any adventurous ingredients, yet the finished product seems like it came right out of a chef's kitchen.

Ingredients:

2 eggs

1/2 avocado

2 slices bruschetta

1 bunch spinach

1 pinch salt

1 pinch pepper

Directions:

1. Start by preheating the toaster oven to 400 degrees.
2. Bring a pan of water to a rolling boil.
3. Place your bruschetta on a pan and toast it in the oven for 10 minutes.
4. Once the water is boiling whisk it around in a circle until it creates a vortex.
5. Drop one egg in the hole and turn the heat to low, poach for 2 minutes.
6. Repeat with the second egg.
7. Mash the avocado and spread it over the toast while your eggs poach.
8. Add the eggs to the toast and top with spinach.

Nutritional Info: Calories: 409, Sodium: 553 mg, Dietary Fiber: 14.2 g, Total Fat: 29.7 g, Total Carbs: 21.7 g, Protein: 22.7 g.

Toasted Banana Cinnamon

Servings: 1 | Prep Time: 10 Minutes | Cook Time: 10 Minutes

These may not be great to look at, but they are another simple recipe that bursts with flavor.

Ingredients:

1 ripe banana	*2 teaspoons honey*
Lemon juice	*Ground cinnamon*

Directions:

1. Start by preheating the toaster oven to 350 degrees.
2. Slice the bananas lengthwise and place them on a greased baking sheet.
3. Brush each slice with lemon juice.
4. Drizzle honey and sprinkle cinnamon over each slice.
5. Bake for 10 minutes.

Nutritional Info: Calories: 154, Sodium: 3 mg, Dietary Fiber: 4.2 g, Total Fat: 0.5 g, Total Carbs: 40.2 g, Protein: 1.5 g.

Toasted Oven Frittata

Servings: 4 | Prep Time: 15 Minutes | Cook Time: 30 Minutes

The only thing more fun than saying frittata is eating one. This recipe creates a whole meal in a single dish and is a great way to start off a parade of amazing toaster oven recipes.

Ingredients:

3 tablespoons olive oil

10 large eggs

2 teaspoons kosher salt

1/2 teaspoon black pepper

1 (5-ounce) bag baby spinach

1 pint grape tomatoes

4 scallions

8 ounces Feta

Directions:

1. Preheat your toaster oven to 350 degrees.

2. Halve your tomatoes and slice your scallions into thin pieces.

3. Add oil to a 2-quart oven safe pan, make sure to brush it onto the sides of the dish as well as the bottom. Place the dish in your toaster oven.

4. Combine the eggs, salt, and pepper in a medium mixing bowl and whisk together for a minute.

5. Add spinach, tomatoes, and scallions to the bowl and mix together until even.

6. Crumble the feta cheese into the bowl and mix together gently. Remove the dish from the oven and pour in the egg mixture.

7. Put the dish back into the oven and bake for 25 – 30 minutes or until the edges of the frittata are browned.

Nutritional Info: Calories: 448, Sodium: 515 mg, Dietary Fiber: 2.3 g, Total Fat: 35.4 g, Total Carbs: 9.3 g, Protein: 25.9 g.

Ultimate Breakfast Burrito

Servings: 8 | Prep Time: 20 Minutes | Prep Time: 20 Minutes

The breakfast burrito is an awesome invention because it allows you to take your breakfast on the go and this recipe is awesome because it takes the breakfast burrito and makes it even better.

Ingredients:

16 ounces cooked bacon ends and pieces

16 eggs

1 tablespoon butter

8 hash browns

8 large soft flour tortillas

2 diced jalapenos

2 cups shredded sharp cheddar

Recipes:

1. If you haven't already cook your bacon pieces.

2. Whisk together eggs in a bowl and set aside.

3. Preheat your toaster oven to 375 degrees.

4. Melt butter into a sauce pan and mix in your eggs until they are starting to cook but not fully hardened.

5. While your eggs are cooking, microwave and cool, your hash brown squares.

6. Roll out your tortillas and top them with hash browns, bacon, jalapenos, and cheese.

7. Wrap the burritos up and place them seem down on a baking sheet.

8. Bake at 375 for 15 – 20 minutes.

Nutritional Info: Calories: 698, Sodium: 1821 mg, Dietary Fiber: 3.4 g, Total Fat: 43.7 g, Total Carbs: 32.9 g, Protein: 42.1 g.

Ultimate Breakfast Sandwich

Servings: 2 | Prep Time: 5 Minutes | Cook Time: 5 Minutes

Pardon the pun, but, breakfast is my jam and there are few breakfast items I enjoy more than a good breakfast sandwich. The only thing better than a good breakfast sandwich is an ultimate breakfast sandwich.

Ingredients:

2 english muffins

2 eggs

2 slices aged yellow cheddar

2 large spicy pork sausage patties

Softened butter

Directions:

1. Start by setting the toaster Black and Decker toaster oven to toast and warming up a non-stick pan.

2. Add sausages to pan and butter the insides of the muffins.

3. While the sausages cook put the muffins in the toaster oven to toast until crispy brown, about 5 – 7 minutes.

4. Set the sausages aside and add eggs to the skillet.

5. Let the whites set, then carefully flip the eggs to keep the yolk intact.

6. Turn off the heat and add cheese and sausage to the top of the egg. This will allow everything to melt together but leave the yolk with the perfect consistency.

7. Add the mixture to the muffin and enjoy the perfect breakfast.

Nutritional Info: Calories: 332, Sodium: 677 mg, Dietary Fiber: 2.0 g, Total Fat: 14.9 g, Total Carbs: 26.1 g, Protein: 22.7 g.

8

Lunch Recipes

10-Minute Rolled Salmon Sandwich

Servings: 1 | Prep Time: 5 Minutes | Cook Time: 5 Minutes

I am not often a fan of fish in any form, but when it tastes like this you'll forget it is fish at all. What a great way to get those important Omega-3s in your diet.

Ingredients:

Piece of flatbread

1 salmon filet

Pinch of salt

1 tablespoon green onion, chopped

1/4 teaspoon dried sumac

1/2 teaspoon thyme

1/2 teaspoon sesame seeds

1/4 english cucumber

1 tablespoon yogurt

Directions:

1. Start by peeling and chopping the cucumber. Cut the salmon at a 45-degree angle in to 4 slices and lay them flat on the flatbread.

2. Sprinkle salmon with salt to taste. Sprinkle onions, thyme, sumac, and sesame seeds evenly over the salmon.

3. Broil the salmon for at least 3 minutes, but more if you want a more well-done fish.

4. While you broil your salmon, mix together the yogurt and cucumber. Remove your flatbread from the toaster oven and put it on a plate, then spoon the yogurt mix over the salmon.

5. Fold the sides of the flatbread in and roll it up for a gourmet lunch that you can take on the go.

Nutritional Info: Calories: 347, Sodium: 397 mg, Dietary Fiber: 1.6 g, Total Fat: 12.4 g, Total Carbs: 20.6 g, Protein: 38.9 g.

Balsamic Roasted Chicken

Servings: 4 | Prep Time: 10 Minutes + Marinade Time | Cook Time: 1 Hour

It doesn't get more gourmet than this; and guess what? All you need is a toaster oven to bake some amazing chicken.

Ingredients:

1/2 cup balsamic vinegar

1/4 cup Dijon mustard

1/3 cup olive oil

Juice and zest from 1 lemon

3 minced garlic cloves

1 teaspoon salt

1 teaspoon pepper

4 bone-in, skin-on chicken thighs

4 bone-in, skin-on chicken drumsticks

1 tablespoon chopped parsley

Directions:

1. Mix vinegar, lemon juice, mustard, olive oil, garlic, salt, and pepper in a bowl then pour into a sauce pan.

2. Roll chicken pieces in the pan then cover and let marinate for at least 2 hours, but up to 24 hours.

3. Preheat the toaster oven to 400 degrees and place the chicken on a fresh baking sheet keeping the marinade for later.

4. Roast the chicken for 50 minutes.

5. Remove the chicken and cover it with foil to keep it warm. Place the marinade in the toaster oven for about 5 minutes until is simmers down and begins to thicken.

6. Pour over chicken and sprinkle with parsley and lemon zest.

Nutritional Info: Calories: 1537, Sodium: 1383 mg, Dietary Fiber: 0.8 g, Total Fat: 70.5 g, Total Carbs: 2.4 g, Protein: 210.4 g.

Chicken Caprese Sandwich

Servings: 2 | Prep Time: 3 Minutes | Cook Time: 3 Minutes

The name sounds a little fancy, and believe me the sandwich is out of this world good, but the truth is it is pretty simple which is great when you are looking for something tasty, but you're short on time.

Ingredients:

2 leftover chicken breast, or pre-cooked breaded chicken

1 large ripe tomato

4 ounces mozzarella cheese slices

4 slices of whole grain bread

1/4 cup olive oil

1/3 cup fresh basil leaves

Salt and pepper to taste

Directions:

1. Start by slicing your tomatoes into thin slices.
2. Layer tomatoes then cheese over two slice of bread and place on a greased baking sheet.
3. Toast in the toaster oven for about 2 minutes or until the cheese is melted.
4. Heat your chicken while the cheese melts.
5. Remove from oven, sprinkle with basil, and add chicken.
6. Drizzle with oil and add salt and pepper.
7. Top with other slices of bread and serve.

Nutritional Info: Calories: 808, Sodium: 847 mg, Dietary Fiber: 5.2 g, Total Fat: 43.6 g, Total Carbs: 30.7 g, Protein: 78.4 g.

Easy Prosciutto Grilled Cheese

Servings: 1 | Prep Time: 5 Minutes | Cook Time: 5 Minutes

Who says that grilled cheese can't be an adult food? This recipe takes grilled cheese to a whole new level, a level that your taste buds won't soon forget.

Ingredients:

2 slices of muenster cheese

2 slices of white bread

Four thinly shaved pieces of prosciutto

1 tablespoon sweet and spicy pickles

Directions:

1. Set your oven on the toast setting.

2. Place your bread flat and put one slice of cheese on each piece of bread.

3. Put Prosciutto on one slice and pickles on the other.

4. Transfer to a baking sheet and toast for 4 minutes or until the cheese is melted.

5. Combine both sides, cut, and serve.

Nutritional Info: Calories: 460, Sodium: 2180 mg, Dietary Fiber: 0 g, Total Fat: 25.2 g, Total Carbs: 11.9 g, Protein: 44.2 g.

Herb Roasted Chicken Tenders

Servings: 2 | Prep Time: 5 Minutes | Cook Time: 10 Minutes

This recipe takes a kid's staple and gives it a little adult flair; your kids will still love them, but you won't need to scramble to find something else to eat.

Ingredients:

7 ounces chicken tenders

1 tablespoon olive oil

1/2 teaspoon herbes de provence

2 tablespoons Dijon mustard

1 tablespoon honey

Salt and pepper

Directions:

1. Start by preheating your toaster oven to 450 degrees.

2. Brush the bottom of a pan with 1/2 tablespoon olive oil.

3. Season the chicken with herbs, salt, and pepper.

4. Place the chicken in a single flat layer in the pan and drizzle the remaining olive oil over it.

5. Bake for about 10 minutes.

6. While the chicken is baking mix together the Dijon and honey for a nice sauce on the side.

Nutritional Info: Calories: 297, Sodium: 268 mg, Dietary Fiber: 0.8 g, Total Fat: 15.5 g, Total Carbs: 9.6 g, Protein: 29.8 g.

Moroccan Pork Kebabs

Servings: 4 | Prep Time: 40 Minutes | Cook Time: 45 Minutes

I have a busy life with a busy family so I usually like to keep my recipes simple, this one is a little heavy on the ingredients side, but it is so worth it in the end.

Ingredients:

1/4 cup orange juice

1 tablespoon tomato paste

1 clove chopped garlic

1 tablespoon ground cumin

1/8 teaspoon ground cinnamon

4 tablespoons olive oil

1 1/2 teaspoons salt

3/4 teaspoons black pepper

1 1/2 pounds boneless pork loin

1 small eggplant

1 small red onion

Pita bread (optional)

1/2 small cucumber

2 tablespoons chopped fresh mint

Wooden skewers

Directions:

1. Start by placing the wooden skewers in water to soak.

2. Cut pork loin and eggplant into 1 to 1 1/2-inches chunks.

3. Preheat your Black and Decker toaster oven to 425 degrees.

4. Cut cucumber and onions into pieces and chop the mint.

5. In a large bowl, combine the orange juice, tomato paste, garlic, cumin, cinnamon, 2 tablespoons of oil, 1 teaspoon of salt, and 1/2 teaspoon of pepper.

6.   Mix in the pork and refrigerate for at least 30 minutes, but up to 8 hours.

7.   Mix together vegetables, remaining oil, and salt and pepper.

8.   Skewer the vegetables and bake them for 20 minutes.

9.   Add the pork to the skewers and bake for an additional 25 minutes.

10.   Remove ingredients from skewer and sprinkle with meat, serve with flatbread if using.

Nutritional Info: Calories: 465, Sodium: 1061 mg, Dietary Fiber: 5.6 g, Total Fat: 20.8 g, Total Carbs: 21.9 g, Protein: 48.2 g.

Oven-Roasted Pecan Crunch Catfish and Asparagus

Servings: 4 | Prep Time: 5 minutes | Cook Time: 12 Minutes

Those who say that catfish isn't edible just don't know how to prepare it. This recipe offers a taste and texture that accent the unique flavor of catfish.

Ingredients:

1 cup whole wheat Panko breadcrumbs

1/4 cup chopped pecans

3 teaspoons chopped fresh thyme

1 1/2 tablespoons extra-virgin olive oil, plus more for the pan

Salt and pepper to taste

1 1/4 pounds asparagus

1 tablespoon honey

4 (5- to 6-ounce each) catfish fillets

Directions:

1. Start by preheating the toaster oven to 425 degrees.

2. Combine breadcrumbs, pecans, 2 teaspoons thyme, 1 tablespoon oil, salt, pepper and 2 tablespoons water.

3. In another bowl put your asparagus, the rest of the thyme, honey, salt, and pepper and toss.

4. Spread the asparagus in a flat layer on a baking sheet. Sprinkle a quarter of the breading over the asparagus.

5. Lay the catfish over the asparagus and press the rest of the breadcrumb mixture into each piece. Roast for 12 minutes.

Nutritional Info: Calories: 531, Sodium: 291 mg, Dietary Fiber: 6.1 g, Total Fat: 30.4 g, Total Carbs: 31.9 g, Protein: 34.8 g.

Parmesan Crusted Pork Loin

Servings: 4 | Prep Time: 10 Minutes | Cook Time: 20 Minutes

In my opinion, pork loin is great no matter how you cook it, but the baked on parmesan crust is the kind of enjoyable meal that the family will be talking about all week.

Ingredients:

1 pound pork loin

1 teaspoon salt

1/2 tablespoon garlic powder

1/2 tablespoon onion powder

2 tablespoons parmesan cheese

1 tablespoon olive oil

Directions:

1. Start by preheating your toaster oven to 475 degrees.

2. Place the pan in the oven and let it heat while the oven preheats.

3. Mix all of the ingredients into a shallow dish and roll the pork loin until it is fully coated.

4. Remove the pan and sear the pork in the pan on each side then bake in the pan for 20 minutes.

Nutritional Info: Calories: 334, Sodium: 718 mg, Dietary Fiber: 0 g, Total Fat: 20.8 g, Total Carbs: 1.7 g, Protein: 33.5 g.

Persimmon Toast with Sour Cream and Cinnamon

Servings: 1 | Prep Time: 5 Minutes | Cook Time: 5 Minutes

You don't find many persimmon recipes, but this one may have you looking for more. It has the perfect taste and texture for a light midmorning or early evening snack.

Ingredients:

1 slice of wheat bread

1/2 persimmon

Sour cream to taste

Sugar to taste

Cinnamon to taste

Directions:

1. Spread a thin layer of sour cream across the bread.
2. Slice the persimmon into 1/4 inch pieces and lay them across the bread.
3. Sprinkle cinnamon and sugar over the persimmon.
4. Toast with your Black and Decker toaster oven until the bread and persimmon begin to brown.

Nutritional Info: Calories: 89, Sodium: 133 mg, Dietary Fiber: 2.0 g, Total Fat: 1.1 g, Total Carbs: 16.5 g, Protein: 3.8 g.

Roasted Beet Salad with Oranges and Beet Greens

Servings: 6 | Prep Time: 1 1/2 hours | Cook Time: 1 1/2 hours

This is a sweet treat for someone who is looking for a substantial snack with a little flavor.

Ingredients:

6 medium beets with beet greens attached	1/4 cup extra-virgin olive oil
2 large oranges	2 mince garlic cloves
1 small sweet onion, cut into wedges	1/2 teaspoon grated orange peel
1/3 cup red wine vinegar	

Directions:

1. Start by preheating the toaster oven to 400 degrees.
2. Trim leaves from beets and chop, then set aside.
3. Pierce beets with a fork and place in a roasting pan.
4. Roast beets for 1 and 1/2 hours.
5. Allow beets to cool, peel, then cut into 8 wedges and put into a bowl.
6. Place beet greens in a sauce pan and cover with just enough water to cover. Heat until boil then immediately remove from heat.
7. Drain greens and press to remove liquid from greens, then add to beet bowl.
8. Remove peel and pith from orange and segment, adding each segment to the bowl.

9.   Add onion to beet mix. In a separate bowl mix together vinegar, oil, garlic and orange peel.

10.   Combine both bowls and toss, sprinkle with salt and pepper.

11.   Let stand for an hour before serving.

Nutritional Info: Calories: 214, Sodium: 183 mg, Dietary Fiber: 6.5 g, Total Fat: 8.9 g, Total Carbs: 32.4 g, Protein: 4.7 g.

Roasted Grape and Goat Cheese Crostinis

Servings: 10 | Prep Time: 30 Minutes | Cook Time: 5 Minutes

I love trying new and weird recipes. Most of them don't make the cut but this one has become one of my favorite new dishes.

Ingredients:

1 pound seedless red grapes

1 teaspoon chopped rosemary

4 tablespoons olive oil

1 rustic French baguette

1 cup sliced shallots

2 tablespoons unsalted butter

8 ounces goat cheese

1 tablespoon honey

Directions:

1. Start by preheating the toaster oven to 400 degrees.
2. Toss grapes, rosemary, and 1 tablespoon of olive oil in a large bowl.
3. Transfer to a roasting pan and roast for 20 minutes.
4. Remove the pan from the oven and set aside to cool.
5. Slice the baguette into 1/2-inch-thick pieces and lay on separate baking sheet.
6. Brush each slice with olive oil and place on baking sheet.
7. Bake for 8 minutes, then remove from oven and set aside.
8. In a medium skillet add butter and one tablespoon of olive oil.
9. Add shallots and sauté for about 10 minutes.
10. Mix goat cheese and honey in a medium bowl, then pour in entire shallot pan and mix thoroughly.

11. Spread shallot mixture onto baguette, top with grapes, and serve.

Nutritional Info: Calories: 238, Sodium: 139 mg, Dietary Fiber: 0.6 g, Total Fat: 16.3 g, Total Carbs: 16.4 g, Protein: 8.4 g.

Roasted Mini Peppers

Servings: 6 | Prep Time: 2 Minutes | Cook Time: 15 Minutes

If you love peppers, then you will eat these things like they are candy. They are super simple to roast and about as healthy of a snack as you can get.

Ingredients:

1 bag mini bell peppers

Cooking spray

Salt and pepper to taste

Directions:

1. Start by preheating your toaster oven to 400 degrees.
2. Wash and dry the peppers then place them flat on a baking sheet.
3. Spray them with cooking spray and sprinkle with salt and pepper.
4. Roast for 15 minutes.

Nutritional Info: Calories: 19, Sodium: 2 mg, Dietary Fiber: 1.3 g, Total Fat: 0.3 g, Total Carbs: 3.6 g, Protein: 0.6 g.

Skinny Black Bean Flautas

Servings: 10 | Prep Time: 10 Minutes | Cook Time: 25 Minutes

Flautas are an excellent for a low calorie snack or a stand out appetizer for a party. They are quick to make and not ingredient heavy so you don't need to put a lot of grocery planning into.

Ingredients:

2 (15-ounce) cans black beans

1 cup shredded cheddar

1 (4-ounce) can diced green chilies

2 teaspoons taco seasoning

10 (8-inch) whole wheat flour tortillas

Olive oil

Directions:

1. Start by preheating your toaster oven to 350 degrees.

2. Drain the black beans, put them in a medium bowl and mash them with a fork.

3. Mix in cheese, chilies, and taco seasoning until all ingredients are even throughout.

4. Evenly spread the mix over each tortilla and wrap tightly.

5. Brush each side lightly with olive oil and place on a baking sheet.

6. Bake for 12 minutes, turn, and bake for another 13 minutes.

Nutritional Info: Calories: 367, Sodium: 136 mg, Dietary Fiber: 14.4 g, Total Fat: 2.8 g, Total Carbs: 64.8 g, Protein: 22.6 g.

Spice Roasted Almonds

Servings: 32 | Prep Time: 5 Minutes | Cook Time: 10 Minutes

Nuts are a great healthy snack, and they have a lot of flavor by themselves. Unfortunately, nuts can get a little bland if you over do them. This recipe breathes new life into this old standard.

Ingredients:

1 tablespoon chili powder

1 tablespoon olive oil

1/2 teaspoon salt

1/2 teaspoon ground cumin

1/2 teaspoon ground coriander

1/4 teaspoon ground cinnamon

1/4 teaspoon black pepper

2 cups whole almonds

Directions:

1. Start by preheating the toaster oven to 350 degrees.
2. Mix olive oil, chili powder, coriander, cinnamon, cumin, salt, and pepper.
3. Add in almonds and toss together.
4. Transfer to a baking pan and bake for 10 minutes.

Nutritional Info: Calories: 39, Sodium: 37 mg, Dietary Fiber: 0.8 g, Total Fat: 3.5 g, Total Carbs: 1.4 g, Protein: 1.3 g.

Sweet Potato and Parsnip Spiralized Latkes

Servings: 12 | Prep Time: 20 Minutes | Cook Time: 20 Minutes

Parsnips have so many health benefits, but the problem is that not many people know what to do with them. When you combine them with sweet potatoes you make a healthy snack that makes everyone happy.

Ingredients:

1 medium sweet potato

1 large parsnip

4 cups water

1 egg + 1 egg white

2 scallions

1/2 teaspoon garlic powder

1/2 teaspoon sea salt

1/2 teaspoon ground pepper

Directions:

1. Start by spiralizing the sweet potato and parsnip and chopping the scallions, only reserving the green parts.

2. Preheat the toaster oven to 425 degrees.

3. Bring 4 cups of water to a boil. Place all of your noodles in a colander and pour the boiling water over the top, draining well.

4. Let the noodles cool, then grab handfuls and place them in a paper towel, squeeze them to remove as much liquid as possible.

5. In a large bowl, beat egg and egg white together. Add noodles, scallions, garlic powder, salt, and pepper, mix well.

6. Prepare a baking sheet and scoop out 1/4 cup of mix at a time and place it on the baking sheet.

7. Press each scoop down slightly with your hands then bake for 20 minutes, flipping half way through.

Nutritional Info: Calories: 24, Sodium: 91 mg, Dietary Fiber: 1.0 g, Total Fat: 0.4 g, Total Carbs: 4.3 g, Protein: 0.9 g.

Sweet Potato Chips

Servings: 2 | Prep Time: 5 Minutes | Cook Time: 40 Minutes

This is a healthy alternative to potato chips, and to be honest, these chips bring a lot more flavor to the table.

Ingredients:

2 sweet potatoes

Olive oil

Salt and pepper to taste

Cinnamon

Directions:

1. Start by preheating your toaster oven to 400 degrees.
2. Cut off each end of the potato and throw them away.
3. Cut the potatoes into 1/2-inch slices.
4. Brush a pan with olive oil and lay slices flat on the pan.
5. Bake for 20 minutes, then flip and bake for another 20.

Nutritional Info: Calories: 139, Sodium: 29 mg, Dietary Fiber: 8.2 g, Total Fat: 0.5 g, Total Carbs: 34.1 g, Protein: 1.9 g.

Toaster Oven Corn Bread

Servings: 12 | Prep Time: 10 Minutes | Cook Time: 20 Minutes

Few foods say country comfort like a good corn bread. This is a simple recipe that brings that country comfort into your home.

Ingredients:

1 cup yellow cornmeal

1 1/2 cups oatmeal

1/4 teaspoon Salt

1/4 cup granulated sugar

2 teaspoons baking powder

1 cup milk

1 large egg

1/2 cup applesauce

Directions:

1. Start by blending the oatmeal into a fine powder.
2. Preheat the toaster oven to 400 degrees.
3. Mix oatmeal, cornmeal, salt, sugar, and baking powder, stir to blend.
4. Add milk, egg, and applesauce, and mix well.
5. Pour into a pan and bake for 20 minutes.

Nutritional Info: Calories: 113, Sodium: 71 mg, Dietary Fiber: 1.9 g, Total Fat: 1.9 g, Total Carbs: 21.5 g, Protein: 3.4 g.

Toaster Oven French Fries

Servings: 1 | Prep Time: 10 Minutes | Cook Time: 30 Minutes

Homemade fries always beat those freezer bag ones. This recipe is awesome not only because they taste great, but because the portion size is perfect.

Ingredients:

1 medium potato

1 tablespoon olive oil

Salt and pepper to taste

Directions:

1. Start by preheating your oven to 425 degrees.
2. Clean the potato and cut it into fries or wedges.
3. Place fries in a bowl of cold water.
4. Dry the fries on a thick sheet of paper towels and pat the tops dry.
5. Toss in a bowl with oil, salt, and pepper.
6. Bake for 30 minutes

Nutritional Info: Calories: 284, Sodium: 13 mg, Dietary Fiber: 4.7 g, Total Fat: 14.2 g, Total Carbs: 37.3 g, Protein: 4.3 g.

Parmigiano Reggiano and Prosciutto Toasts with Balsamic Glaze

Servings: 8 | Prep Time: 25 Minutes | Cook Time: 15 Minutes

This entrée may be hard to say, but it sure does taste great. People will never believe that you cooked this meal in a toaster oven.

Ingredients:

3 ounces thinly sliced prosciutto, cut crosswise into 1/4-inch-wide strips

1 (3-ounce) piece Parmigiano Reggiano cheese

1/2 cup balsamic vinegar

1 medium red onion, thinly sliced

1 loaf ciabatta, cut into 3/4-inch-thick slices

1 tablespoon extra-virgin olive oil

1 clove garlic

Black pepper to taste

Directions:

1. Preheat your toaster oven to 350 degrees.

2. Place the onion in a bowl of cold water and let sit for 10 minutes.

3. Bring your vinegar to a boil, then reduce heat and simmer for 5 minutes.

4. Remove from heat completely and set aside to allow the vinegar to thicken.

5. Drain the onion.

6. Brush the tops of each bun with oil, rub with garlic, and sprinkle with pepper.

7. Use a vegetable peeler to make large curls of Parmigiano

8. Reggiano and place them on the bun.

9.   Bake for 15 minutes or until the bread just starts to crisp.

10.   Sprinkle prosciutto and onions on top, then drizzle vinegar and
        serve.

Nutritional Info: Calories: 154, Sodium: 432 mg, Dietary Fiber: 1.0 g, Total Fat: 5.6 g,
Total Carbs: 17.3 g, Protein: 8.1 g.

Philly Cheesesteak Eggrolls

Servings: 4 -5 | Prep Time: 20 Minutes | Cook Time: 20 Minutes

Who doesn't love a good cheesesteak? The only negative part about a cheesesteak is that they can get a little messy. That is all fixed when you slide those ingredients into an easily portable eggroll.

Ingredients:

1 egg

1 tablespoons milk

2 tablespoons olive oil

1 small red onion

1 small red bell pepper

1 small green bell pepper

1 pound thinly slice roast beef

8 ounces shredded pepper jack cheese

8 ounces shredded provolone cheese

8-10 egg roll skins

Salt and pepper

Directions:

1. Start by preheating your Black and Decker toaster oven to 425 degrees.

2. Mix together you egg in milk in a shallow bowl and set it aside for later use.

3. Chop your onions and bell peppers into small pieces.

4. Heat the oil in a medium sauce pan and add the onions and peppers.

5. Cook the onions and peppers for 2 – 3 minutes until they are softened.

6. Add roast beef to the pan and sauté for another 5 minutes.

7. Add salt and pepper to taste.

8. Add cheese and mix together until melted.

9. Remove from heat and drain liquid from pan.

10. Roll the egg roll skins flat.

11. Add equal parts of the mix to each egg roll and roll them up per the instructions on the package.

12. Brush each eggroll with the egg mix.

13. Line a pan with parchment paper and leg eggrolls seam side down with a gap between each roll.

14. Bake for 20 – 25 minutes depending on your preference of eggroll crispness.

Nutritional Info: Calories: 769, Sodium: 1114 mg, Dietary Fiber: 2.1 g, Total Fat: 39.9 g, Total Carbs: 41.4 g, Protein: 58.4 g.

Portobello Pesto Burgers

Servings: 4 | Prep Time: 10 Minutes | Cook Time: 26 Minutes

This is an excellent vegetarian—not vegan—meal that is easy to prepare and proves that going vegetarian doesn't mean leaving the flavor behind.

Ingredients:

4 portobello mushrooms

1/4 cup sun-dried-tomato pesto

4 whole-grain hamburger buns

1 large ripe tomato

1 log fresh goat cheese

8 large fresh basil leaves

Directions:

1. Start by preheating your toaster oven to 425 degrees.
2. Place the mushrooms on a pan round side facing up.
3. Bake for 14 minutes.
4. Pull out tray, flip the mushrooms and spread 1 tablespoon of pesto on each piece.
5. Return to oven and bake for another 10 minutes.
6. Remove the mushrooms and toast the buns for 2 minutes.
7. Remove the buns and build the burger by placing tomatoes, mushroom, 2 slices of cheese, and a sprinkle of basil, then topping with the top bun.

Nutritional Info: Calories: 297, Sodium: 346 mg, Dietary Fiber: 1.8 g, Total Fat: 18.1 g, Total Carbs: 19.7 g, Protein: 14.4 g.

Roasted Delicata Squash with Kale

Servings: 2 | Prep Time: 5 Minutes | Cook Time: 10 Minutes

The idea that the toaster oven is a substandard cooking device goes right out the kitchen window when you can cook a high class meal like this one.

Ingredients:

1 medium delicata squash

1 bunch kale

1 clove garlic

2 tablespoons olive oil

Salt and pepper

Directions:

1. Start by preheating your toaster oven to 425 degrees.

2. Clean the squash and cut off each end. Cut the squash in half and ball out the seeds. Quarter the halves.

3. Toss the squash in 1 tablespoon of olive oil.

4. Place the squash on a greased baking sheet and roast for 25 Minutes, turning half way through.

5. Rinse kale and remove stems. Chop Garlic.

6. Heat the leftover oil in a medium skillet and add kale and salt to taste.

7. Sauté the kale until it darkens then mix in the garlic.

8. Cook for another minute then remove from heat and add 2 tablespoons of water.

9. Remove squash from oven and lay it on top of the garlic kale.

10. Top with salt and pepper to taste and serve.

Nutritional Info: Calories: 159, Sodium: 28 mg, Dietary Fiber: 1.8 g, Total Fat: 14.2 g, Total Carbs: 8.2 g, Protein: 2.6 g.

Seven Layer Tostadas

Servings: 6 | Prep Time: 15 Minutes | Cook Time: 5 Minutes

In the mood for Mexican but don't want a boring old taco? A tostada is like a taco pizza and is a great meal for one or appetizer at a party.

Ingredients:

1 (16-ounce) can refried pinto beans

1 1/2 cups guacamole

1 cup light sour cream

1/2 teaspoon taco seasoning

1 cup shredded mexican cheese blend

1 cup chopped tomatoes

1/2 cup thinly sliced green onions

1/2 cup sliced black olives

6-8 whole wheat flour tortillas small enough to fit your oven

Olive oil

Directions:

1. Start by placing baking sheet into your toaster oven while you preheat it to 450 degrees. Remove pan and drizzle with olive oil.

2. Place tortillas on pan and cook in oven until they are crisp, turn at least once, this should take about 5 minutes or less.

3. Put your refried beans in a medium bowl and mash them up to break apart any chunks and microwave them for 2 1/2 minutes.

4. Stir your taco seasoning into the sour cream. Chop your vegetables and halve your olives.

5. Add your ingredients in this order, refried beans, guacamole, sour cream, shredded cheese, tomatoes, onions, and olives.

Nutritional Info: Calories: 657, Sodium: 581 mg, Dietary Fiber: 16.8 g, Total Fat: 31.7 g, Total Carbs: 71.3 g, Protein: 28.9 g.

Shrimp and Roasted Fennel Ditalini

Servings: 4 | Prep Time: 40 Minutes | Cook Time: 30 Minutes

Even shrimp can be made in a toaster oven, and the oven actually gives it a really nice baked texture; add a little pasta and you have a complete gourmet meal.

Ingredients:

1 pound extra-large, thawed, tail on shrimp

1 teaspoon fennel seeds

1 teaspoon salt

1 fennel bulb, halved and sliced crosswise

4 chopped cloves garlic

2 tablespoons olive oil

1/2 teaspoon freshly ground black pepper

Grated zest of 1 lemon

1/2 pound whole-wheat ditalini

Directions:

1.   Start by preheating the toaster oven to 450 degrees.

2.   Toast the seeds in a medium pan over medium heat for about 5 minutes, then toss with shrimp.

3.   Add water and 1/2 teaspoon salt to the pan and bring the mixture to a boil.

4.   Reduce heat and simmer for 30 minutes.

5.   Combine fennel, garlic, oil, pepper, and remaining salt in a roasting pan.

6.   Roast for 20 minutes, then add shrimp mix and roast for another 5 minutes or until shrimp are cooked.

7.   While the fennel is roasting cook your pasta per the directions on the package, drain, and set aside.

8. Remove the Shrimp mixture and mix in pasta, roast for another 5 minutes.

Nutritional Info: Calories: 420, Sodium: 890 mg, Dietary Fiber: 4.2 g, Total Fat: 10.2 g, Total Carbs: 49.5 g, Protein: 33.9 g.

Spicy Avocado Cauliflower Toast

Servings: 2 | Prep Time: 45 Minutes | Cook Time: 15 Minutes

I'm not going to lie, this one takes some time and work, but the results are definitely worth the effort.

Ingredients:

1/2 a large head of cauliflower with leaves removed

3 1/4 teaspoons olive oil

1 small jalapeño

1 tablespoon chopped cilantro leaves

2 slices whole grain bread

1 medium avocado

Salt and pepper

5 radishes

1 green onion

2 teaspoons hot sauce

1 lime

Directions:

1. Start by preheating the toaster oven to 450 degrees.

2. Cut the cauliflower into thick pieces, about 3/4 inches, and slice the jalapeno into thin slices.

3. Place the cauliflower and jalapeno in a bowl and mix together with 2 teaspoons olive oil.

4. Add salt and pepper to taste and mix for another minute.

5. Coat a pan with another teaspoon of olive oil then lay the cauliflower mixture flat across the pan.

6. Cook for 20 minutes, flipping in the last 5 minutes.

7. Reduce heat to toast.

8. Sprinkle cilantro over the mix while it is still warm, and set aside.

9. Brush bread with remaining oil and toast until golden brown, about 5 minutes.

10. Dice onion and radish

11. Mash avocado in a bowl, then spread on toast and sprinkle salt and pepper to taste.

12. Put cauliflower mix on toast and cover with onion and radish. Drizzle with hot sauce and serve with a lime wedge.

Nutritional Info: Calories: 359, Sodium: 308 mg, Dietary Fiber: 11.1 g, Total Fat: 28.3 g, Total Carbs: 26.4 g, Protein: 6.6 g.

Squash and Zucchini Mini Pizza

Servings: 4 | Prep Time: 25 Minutes | Cook Time: 15 Minutes

This recipe is the perfect combination of happy and healthy. It is packed with healthy vegetables, but doesn't taste like health food.

Ingredients:

1 crust

1/2 cup parmesan cheese

4 tablespoons oregano

1 zucchini

1 yellow summer squash

Olive oil

Salt and pepper

Directions:

1. Start by preheating your toaster oven to 350 degrees.

2. If you are using homemade crust roll out 8 mini portions, if it is store bought use a cookie cutter to cut out the portions.

3. Sprinkle Parmesan and oregano equally on each piece. Layer the zucchini and squash in a circle – one on top of the other – around the entire circle.

4. Brush with olive oil and sprinkle salt and pepper to taste.

5. Bake for 15 minutes and serve.

Nutritional Info: Calories: 151, Sodium: 327 mg, Dietary Fiber: 3.1 g, Total Fat: 8.6 g, Total Carbs: 10.3 g, Protein: 11.4 g.

Toaster Oven Butter Fish

Servings: 4 | Prep Time: 15 Minutes + Marinade Time | Cook Time: 11 Minutes

Many people don't realize that you can use a toaster oven to cook fish, in fact you can use it to cook some of the most delicious fish you will ever have.

Ingredients:

4 (7-ounce) pieces of butter fish

1/3 cup sake

1/3 cup mirin

2/3 cups sugar

1 cup white miso

Directions:

1. Start by combining sake, mirin, and sugar in a sauce pan and bringing the ingredients to a boil.

2. Allow to boil for 5 minutes, then reduce heat and simmer for another 10 minutes.

3. Remove from heat completely and mix in miso.

4. Marinade the fish in the mixture for as long as possible, up to 3 days if you can.

5. Preheat toaster oven to 450 degrees and bake for 8 minutes.

6. Switch your setting to broil and broil the fish for another 2 -3 minutes until the sauce is caramelized.

Nutritional Info: Calories: 529, Sodium: 2892 mg, Dietary Fiber: 3.7 g, Total Fat: 5.8 g, Total Carbs: 61.9 g, Protein: 53.4 g.

Toaster Oven Chicken Breast

Servings: 4 | Prep Time: 10 Minutes | Cook Time: 60 Minutes

Sometimes it is the simpler dishes that are the best as proven by these delicious and juicy chicken breasts.

Ingredients:

4 bone-in chicken breast halves

3 tablespoons softened butter

1/2 teaspoon salt

1/4 teaspoon pepper

1 tablespoon rosemary

1 tablespoon extra-virgin olive oil

Directions:

1. Start by preheating the toaster oven to 400 degrees.
2. Mix the butter, salt, pepper, and rosemary in a bowl.
3. Coat the breasts with the butter and put them in a shallow pan.
4. Drizzle oil over the breasts and roast for 25 minutes.
5. Flip the chicken and roast for another 20 minutes.
6. Flip the chicken one more time and roast for a final 15 minutes.

Nutritional Info: Calories: 392, Sodium: 551 mg, Dietary Fiber: 0 g, Total Fat: 18.4 g, Total Carbs: 0.6 g, Protein: 55.4 g.

Toaster Oven Croque Monsieur

Servings: 2 | Prep Time: 5 Minutes | Cook Time: 13 Minutes

It may just be a fancy ham and cheese sandwich, but it is one spectacular fancy ham and cheese sandwich.

Ingredients:

4 slices of white bread

2 tablespoons unsalted butter

1 tablespoon all-purpose flour

1/2 cup whole milk

3/4 cups shredded Swiss cheese

1/4 teaspoon freshly ground black pepper

1/8 teaspoon salt

1 tablespoon Dijon mustard

4 slices ham

Directions:

1.   Start by cutting the crusts off the bread and placing them on a pan lined with parchment paper.

2.   Melt the 1 tablespoon of butter in a sauce pan then tab the top sides of each piece of bread with butter.

3.   Toast the bread in your oven for 3 -5 minutes until each piece is golden brown.

4.   Melt the second tablespoon of butter in the sauce pan and add the flour, mix together until they form a paste.

5.   Add the milk and continue to mix until the sauce begins to thicken.

6.   Remove from heat and mix in 1 tablespoon of Swiss cheese, salt, and pepper; continue stirring until cheese is melted.

7. Flip the bread over on the pans so the untoasted side is facing up.

8. Set 2 slices aside and spread Dijon on the other two slices.

9. Add ham and sprinkle 1/4 cup Swiss over each piece.

10. Broil for about 3 minutes.

11. Top the sandwiches off with the other slices of bread, soft side down.

12. Top with sauce and sprinkle with remaining Swiss. Toast for another 5 minutes or until the cheese is golden brown.

13. Serve immediately.

Nutritional Info: Calories: 452, Sodium: 1273 mg, Dietary Fiber: 1.6 g, Total Fat: 30.5 g, Total Carbs: 19.8 g, Protein: 24.4 g.

Toaster Oven Pita Melts

Servings: 2 | Prep Time: 10 Minutes | Cook Time: 5 Minutes

This is the kind of recipe that seems like someone, one day, said I want to do something a little different. That day a delicious lunch sandwich was born and now you too can enjoy it.

Ingredients:

2 (6-inch) whole wheat pitas

1 teaspoon extra-virgin olive oil

1 cup grated part-skim mozzarella cheese

1/4 small red onion

1/4 cup pitted Kalamata olives

2 tablespoons chopped fresh herbs such as parsley, basil, or oregano

Directions:

1. Start by preheating your toaster oven to 425 degrees.

2. Brush the pita on both sides with oil and warm in the oven for one minute.

3. Dice onions and halve olives.

4. Sprinkle mozzarella over each pita and top with onion and olive.

5. Return to the oven for another 5 minutes or until the cheese is melted.

6. Sprinkle chosen herbs over the pita and serve.

Nutritional Info: Calories: 387, Sodium: 828 mg, Dietary Fiber: 7.4 g, Total Fat: 16.2 g, Total Carbs: 42.0 g, Protein: 23.0 g.

Toaster Oven Tofu

Servings: 4 | Prep Time: 1 Hour | Cook Time: 45 Minutes

Most people find tofu to be bland and boring, but I see it as a blank slate that you can dress up any way you can imagine. This one takes a little time, but it is well worth it in the taste department and ludicrously simple to make.

Ingredients:

1 or more (16-ounce) containers extra-firm tofu

1 tablespoon sesame oil

1 tablespoon soy sauce

1 tablespoon rice vinegar

1 tablespoon water

Directions:

1. Start by drying the tofu, first pat dry with paper towels, then lay on another set of paper towels or even a dish towel.

2. Put a plate on top of the tofu then put something heavy on the plate (like a large can of vegetables.) Leave it there for as long as you can, but at least 20 minutes.

3. While tofu is being pressed whip up marinade by combining oil, soy sauce, vinegar, and water in a bowl and set aside.

4. Cut the tofu into squares or sticks. Place the tofu in the marinade for at least 30 minutes.

5. Preheat your toaster oven to 350 degrees. Line a pan with parchment paper and add as many pieces of tofu as you can while giving each piece adequate shape.

6. Bake for 20 – 45 minutes, it is done when the outside edges look golden brown. Time will vary depending on tofu size and shape.

Nutritional Info: Calories: 114, Sodium: 239 mg, Dietary Fiber: 1.1 g, Total Fat: 8.1 g, Total Carbs: 2.2 g, Protein: 9.5 g.

Toaster Oven Turkey Stuffed Peppers

Servings: 6 | Prep Time: 20 Minutes | Cook Time: 35 Minutes

Just the name of this meal makes your mouth start to water and just wait until the smell starts to fill your kitchen. There are so many flavors combined in this recipe and they each complement each other perfectly.

Ingredients:

- 1 pound lean ground turkey meat
- 1 tablespoon olive oil
- 2 cloves garlic
- 1/3 onion
- 1 tablespoon cilantro (optional)
- 1 teaspoon garlic powder
- 1 teaspoon cumin powder
- 1/2 teaspoon salt
- Pepper to taste
- 3 large red bell peppers
- 1 cup chicken broth
- 1/4 cup tomato sauce
- 1 1/2 cups cooked brown rice
- 1/4 cup shredded cheddar
- 6 green onions

Directions:

1. Start by preheating your toaster oven to 400 degrees.
2. Heat a skillet on medium heat and mince onion and garlic.
3. Add olive oil to the skillet, then mix in onion and garlic.
4. Sauté for about 5 minutes or until the onion stars to look opaque.
5. Add the turkey to the skillet and season with cumin, garlic powder, salt, and pepper.
6. Brown the meat until thoroughly cooked, then mix in chicken broth and tomato sauce.

7.   Reduce heat and simmer for about 5 minutes, stirring occasionally.

8.   Add the brown rice and continue stirring until it is evenly spread through the mix.

9.   Cut the bell peppers lengthwise down the middle and remove all of the seeds.

10. Grease a pan or line it with parchment paper and lay all peppers in the pan with the outside facing down.

11. Spoon the meat mixture evenly into each pepper and use the back of the spoon to level it out.

12. Bake for 30 minutes.

13. Pull the pan out and sprinkle cheddar over each pepper and put it back in for another 3 minutes or until the cheese is melted.

14. While the cheese melts, dice your green onions. Remove the pan from the oven and sprinkle the diced green onions over each pepper and serve.

Nutritional Info: Calories: 394, Sodium: 493 mg, Dietary Fiber: 4.1 g, Total Fat: 12.9 g, Total Carbs: 44.4 g, Protein: 27.7 g.

Tomato Avocado Melt

Servings: 2 | Prep Time: 5 Minutes | Cook Time: 4 Minutes

This recipe is all kinds of amazing and will surely become a family favorite in your home. It is light, quick, and delicious on top of being relatively healthy.

Ingredients:

4 slices of bread

1-2 tablespoon mayonnaise

Cayenne pepper

1 small roma tomato

1/2 avocado

8 slices of cheese

Directions:

1. Start by slicing your avocado and tomato and set them aside.

2. Spread mayonnaise on the bread.

3. Sprinkle cayenne pepper toaster over the mayo to taste.

4. Layer tomato and avocado on top of each other.

5. Top with cheese and put on greased baking sheet.

6. Broil on high for 2 – 4 minutes until the cheese is melted and bread is toasted.

Nutritional Info: Calories: 635, Sodium: 874 mg, Dietary Fiber: 4.1 g, Total Fat: 50.1 g, Total Carbs: 17.4 g, Protein: 30.5 g.

Vegetarian Philly Sandwich

Servings: 2 | Prep Time: 5 Minutes | Cook Time: 20 Minutes

If meat isn't your thing it doesn't mean that you should miss out on an American staple. This recipe has all of the flavor, but none of the You Know What.

Ingredients:

2 tablespoons olive oil

8 ounces sliced Portabella mushrooms

1 vidalia onion

1 green bell pepper

1 red bell pepper

Salt and Pepper

4 slices 2% provolone cheese

4 rolls

Directions:

1. Start by slicing your peppers and onion into thin slices.

2. Preheat the toaster oven to 475 degrees.

3. Heat the oil in a medium sauce over medium heat.

4. Sauté mushrooms by themselves for about 5 minutes, then add the onions and peppers and sauté for another 10 minutes.

5. Open the rolls and divide the vegetables into each roll.

6. Add the cheese and toast until the rolls start to brown and the cheese melts.

Nutritional Info: Calories: 645, Sodium: 916 mg, Dietary Fiber: 7.2 g, Total Fat: 33.3 g, Total Carbs: 61.8 g, Protein: 27.1 g.

9

Dinner Recipes

Baked Veggie Eggrolls

Servings: 2 | Prep Time: 10 Minutes | Cook Time: 20 Minutes

Who doesn't love a good eggroll? Not only do these eggrolls taste great, but they are a great vegetarian option.

Ingredients:

1/2 tablespoon olive or vegetable oil

2 cups thinly-sliced chard

1/4 cup grated carrot

1/2 cup chopped pea pods

3 shiitake mushrooms

2 scallions

2 medium cloves garlic

1/2 tablespoon fresh ginger

1/2 tablespoon soy sauce

6 eggroll wrappers

Olive oil spray for cookie sheet and eggrolls

Directions:

1. Start by mincing mushrooms, garlic, and ginger and slicing scallions.

2. Heat oil on medium heat in a medium skillet and char, peas, carrots, scallions, and mushrooms.

3. Cook for 3 minutes then add ginger. Stir in soy sauce and remove from heat.

4. Preheat the toaster oven to 400 degrees and spray the cookie sheet. Spoon even portions of vegetable mix over each eggroll and wrap them up.

5. Place eggrolls on cookie sheet and spray with olive oil. Bake for 20 minutes until eggroll shells are browned.

Nutritional Info: Calories: 421, Sodium: 1166 mg, Dietary Fiber: 8.2 g, Total Fat: 7.7 g, Total Carbs: 76.9 g, Protein: 13.7 g.

Broccoli and Avocado Tacos

Servings: 3 | Prep Time: 25 Minutes | Cook Time: 5 Minutes

It is rare to find the words delicious, vegan, and gluten free in the same sentence, but here they are. This is an amazing entrée that meets all of those requirements and is easy to throw together in a short period of time.

Ingredients:

6-10 authentic mexican corn tortillas

1 large ripe avocado

1 large head broccoli

6-8 simple white mushrooms

1/2 bunch cilantro

1/2 teaspoon garlic powder

Sea salt and pepper

Olive oil

Directions:

1. Start by preheating your Black and Decker toaster oven to 400 degrees.

2. Slice avocado into thin slices and chop the broccoli into bite-sized florets.

3. Arrange the broccoli and mushrooms on a baking sheet and drizzle oil and sprinkle salt, pepper, and garlic powder over the veggies.

4. Bake them for 20 minutes. Warm the tortillas on a flat top and fill with mushrooms and broccoli, and top with avocado.

5. Sprinkle cilantro over the tacos and serve.

Nutritional Info: Calories: 313, Sodium: 99 mg, Dietary Fiber: 12.6 g, Total Fat: 15.3 g, Total Carbs: 40.5 g, Protein: 10.4 g.

Broiled Tilapia with Parmesan and Herbs

Servings: 4 | Prep Time: 25 Minutes | Cook Time: 8 Minutes

Tilapia is a great fish to cook with because its mild flavor goes well in many recipes like this one where the tilapia is the main dish but the parmesan and herbs take center stage in the flavor.

Ingredients:

4 (6 to 8 ounce) farm-raised tilapia fillets

1/2 cup freshly grated parmesan cheese

2 tablespoons low fat mayonnaise

2 tablespoons light sour cream

2 tablespoons melted unsalted butter

2 tablespoons juice

1/2 teaspoon dried basil

1/2 teaspoon dried tarragon

1/8 teaspoon onion powder

Salt and pepper to taste

Directions:

1. Mix together 1/4 cup parmesan and all other ingredients, except tilapia.

2. Place the mixture in a plastic zipper bag, add fish and toss.

3. Place fish in a shallow pan and set aside to marinate for 20 minutes.

4. Place the fish in a broiler pan and top with a few spoonful of marinade and sprinkle the rest of the parmesan over the fish.

5. Broil until lightly browned, around 8 minutes.

Nutritional Info: Calories: 369, Sodium: 459 mg, Dietary Fiber: 0 g, Total Fat: 17.7 g, Total Carbs: 2.0 g, Protein: 51.6 g.

Coconut Crusted Haddock with Curried Pumpkin Seeds

Serve: 4 | Prep Time: 20 Minutes | Cook Time: 10 Minutes

One of the hardest parts of eating healthy is to find foods that don't taste like "health foods." This recipe does a great job at keeping the calories low, but letting the flavor fly.

Ingredients:

- 2 teaspoons canola oil
- 2 teaspoons honey
- 1 teaspoon curry powder
- 1/4 teaspoon ground cinnamon
- 1 teaspoon salt
- 1 cup pumpkin seeds
- 1 1/2 pounds haddock or cod fillets
- 1/2 cup roughly grated unsweetened coconut
- 3/4 cups panko-style bread crumbs
- 2 tablespoons butter, melted
- 3 tablespoons apricot fruit spread
- 1 tablespoon lime juice

Directions:

1. Start by preheating the toaster oven to 350 degrees.
2. In a medium bowl, mix honey, oil, curry powder, 1/2 teaspoon salt, and cinnamon.
3. Add pumpkin seeds to the bowl and toss to coat, then lay them flat on a baking sheet.
4. Toast for 14 minutes, then transfer to a bowl to cool.
5. Increase the oven temperature to 450 degrees.
6. Brush a baking sheet with oil and lay haddock pieces flat.

7.   In another medium mixing bowl, mix together bread crumbs, butter, and remaining salt.

8.   In a small bowl mash together apricot spread and lime juice.

9.   Brush each haddock piece with apricot then press bread crumb mixture onto each piece.

10.   Bake for 10 minutes.

11.   Transfer to a plate and top with pumpkin seeds to serve.

Nutritional Info: Calories: 273, Sodium: 491 mg, Dietary Fiber: 6.1 g, Total Fat: 8.4 g, Total Carbs: 47.3 g, Protein: 7.0 g.

Herbed Oven-Fried Chicken

Servings: 2 | Prep Time: 10 Minutes + Marinate Time | Cook Time: 15 Minutes

This recipe screams comfort food and offers that crunch that we love with our chicken. The best part is that there is nothing complicated about it, there are just a few steps between you and perfect flavor.

Ingredients:

1/2 cup buttermilk

2 cloves minced garlic

1 1/2 teaspoons salt

1 tablespoon oil

1/2 pound boneless, skinless chicken breasts

1 cup rolled oats

1/2 teaspoon red pepper flakes

1/2 cup grated parmesan cheese

1/4 cup fresh basil leaves or rosemary needles

Olive oil spray

Directions:

1. Mix together buttermilk, oil, 1/2 teaspoon salt, and garlic in a shallow bowl.

2. Roll the chicken in the buttermilk and leave in the bowl, refrigerate overnight.

3. Preheat your Black and Decker toaster oven to 425 degrees.

4. Mix together the oats, red pepper, salt, parmesan, and basil, mix roughly to break up oats.

5. Place the mixture on a plate.

6. Remove the chicken from the buttermilk mixture and let any excess drip off.

7. Roll the chicken in the oat mix and transfer to a baking sheet that you have sprayed with olive oil spray.

8. Spray the chicken with oil spray and bake for 15 minutes.

Nutritional Info: Calories: 651, Sodium: 713 mg, Dietary Fiber: 4.4 g, Total Fat: 31.2 g, Total Carbs: 34.1 g, Protein: 59.5 g.

Miso Glazed Salmon

Servings: 4 | Prep Time: 10 Minutes | Cook Time: 5 Minutes

This is another case of cooking gourmet fish in a toaster oven. It may seem questionable, but the results are always worth the trial.

Ingredients:

1/4 cup red or white miso

1/3 cup sake

1 tablespoon soy sauce

2 tablespoons vegetable oil

1/4 cup sugar

4 skinless salmon filets

Directions:

1. In a shallow bowl, mix together the miso, sake, oil, soy sauce, and sugar.

2. Toss the salmon in the mixture until thoroughly coated on all sides and transfer to a plastic bag.

3. Preheat your toaster oven to high on broil mode.

4. Place the salmon in a broiling pan and broil until the top is well charred—about 5 minutes.

Nutritional Info: Calories: 401, Sodium: 315 mg, Dietary Fiber: 0 g, Total Fat: 19.2 g, Total Carbs: 14.1 g, Protein: 39.2 g.

Pesto Salmon

Servings: 4 | Prep Time: 20 Minutes | Cook Time: 10 Minutes

This is another entry in the category of fish too delicious to actually be called fish. It is simple to make and will win over even the most staunch fish hater.

Ingredients:

1 1/4 pounds salmon filet

2 tablespoons white wine

2 tablespoons pesto

1 lemon

Directions:

1. Cut the salmon into 4 pieces and place on a greased baking sheet.

2. Slice the lemon into quarters and squeeze 1 quarter over each piece of salmon.

3. Drizzle wine over salmon and set aside to marinate while you preheat the toaster oven on broil.

4. Spread pesto over each piece of salmon.

5. Broil for at least 10 minutes or until the fish is cooked to your liking and the pesto is browned.

Nutritional Info: Calories: 236, Sodium: 111 mg, Dietary Fiber: 0.9 g, Total Fat: 12.1 g, Total Carbs: 3.3 g, Protein: 28.6 g.

Rigatoni with Roasted Broccoli and Chick Peas

Servings: 4 | Prep Time: 30 Minutes | Cook Time: 10 Minutes

There is no shortage of pasta recipes out there but most of them are just pasta and sauce. This vegetarian recipe lets the pasta shine without a heavy sauce.

Ingredients:

1 can anchovies packed in oil

4 cloves chopped garlic

1 can chickpeas

1 chicken bouillon cube

1 pound broccoli, cut into small florets

1/2 pound whole-wheat rigatoni

1/2 cup grated romano

Directions:

1. Start by chopping the anchovies and cutting the broccoli into small florets.

2. Set the anchovy oil aside for later use.

3. Preheat your Black and Decker toaster oven to 450 degrees.

4. In a shallow sauce pan, sauté the anchovies in the oil with garlic until the garlic browns.

5. Drain the chickpeas, but be sure to save the canned liquid.

6. Add the chickpea liquid and bullion to the anchovies, stir until bullion dissolves.

7. Pour anchovy mix into a roasting pan and add broccoli and chickpeas.

8. Roast for 20 minutes.

9.   While the veggies roast cook rigatoni per the package directions, drain the pasta saving one cup of water.

10.   Add the pasta to the anchovy mix and roast for another 10 minutes add liquid and stirring a little at a time until the pasta reaches your desired consistency.

11.   Top with Romano and serve.

Nutritional Info: Calories: 574, Sodium: 1198 mg, Dietary Fiber: 13.7 g, Total Fat: 14.0 g, Total Carbs: 81.1 g, Protein: 31.1 g.

Roasted Butternut Squash with Brussels Sprouts and Sweet Potato Noodles

Servings: 2 | Prep Time: 2 Hours 30 Minutes | Cook Time: 15 Minutes

This is another one of those recipes that proves that vegan doesn't mean tasteless. This flavorful dish takes a bit of prep work, but is well worth it and a health alternative for the entire family.

Ingredients:

Squash:

3 cups chopped butternut squash	2 teaspoons extra light olive oil
	1/8 teaspoon sea salt

Veggies:

5-6 brussels sprouts	A small pinch red pepper flakes
5 fresh shiitake mushrooms	1 tablespoon extra light olive oil
2 cloves garlic	1 teaspoon sesame oil
1/2 teaspoon black sesame seeds	1 teaspoon onion powder
1/2 teaspoon white sesame seeds	1 teaspoon garlic powder
A few sprinkles ground pepper	1/4 teaspoon sea salt

Noodles:

1 bundle sweet potato vermicelli

2-3 teaspoons low sodium soy sauce

Directions:

1. Start by soaking your potato vermicelli in water, this takes at least 2 hours.

2. Preheat your toaster oven to 375 degrees.

3. Place squash on a baking sheet with edges, drizzle olive oil and sprinkle with salt and pepper. Mix together well on pan.

4. Bake the squash for 30 minutes, mixing and flipping half way through.

5. Remove the stems from the mushrooms and chop the Brussels sprouts.

6. Chop garlic and mix the veggies.

7. Drizzle sesame and olive oil over the mix then add garlic powder, onion powder, sesame seeds, red pepper flakes, salt, and pepper.

8. Bake this veggie mix for 15 minutes.

9. While the veggies bake, put your noodles in a small sauce pan and add just enough water to cover them.

10. Bring the water to a rolling boil and boil for about 8 minutes.

11. Drain the noodles and combine with the squash and veggies in a large bowl.

12. Drizzle with soy sauce, sprinkle with sesame seeds, and serve.

Nutritional Info: Calories: 409, Sodium: 1124 mg, Dietary Fiber: 12.2 g, Total Fat: 15.6 g, Total Carbs: 69.3 g, Protein: 8.8 g.

Spicy Honey Chicken

Servings: 4 | Prep Time: 40 Minutes + Marinate Time | Cook Time: 30 Minutes

This recipe is a great way to add a little flair to dinner with a bit of sugar, spice, and everything nice.

Ingredients:

1 package of chicken thighs/wings

1 tablespoon sugar

1 1/3 tablespoons chili garlic sauce

1/4 cup soy sauce

1 tablespoon sesame oil

1 tablespoon ketchup

1 tablespoon honey

1 tablespoon soy sauce

1 teaspoon brown sugar or sugar

1 teaspoon cornstarch

Directions:

1. Create a marinade by combining 1 tablespoon chili sauce, soy sauce, and sesame oil.

2. Toss the chicken in the marinade and refrigerate for at least 30 minutes, but up to a day.

3. Preheat the toaster oven to 375 degrees. Place the chicken on a baking sheet with a little space between each piece and bake for 30 minutes.

4. While the chicken bakes create the sauce by combining all the leftover ingredients including the 1/3 tablespoon of chili sauce.

5. Mix well and microwave in 30-second intervals until the sauce starts to thicken.

6. Toss the chicken in the sauce and serve.

Nutritional Info: Calories: 401, Sodium: 1439 mg, Dietary Fiber: 0 g, Total Fat: 16.0 g, Total Carbs: 11.2 g, Protein: 50.6 g.

Tex-Mex Chicken Quesadillas

Servings: 4 | Prep Time: 10 Minutes | Cook Time: 10 Minutes

Quesadillas are like pizza, everyone loves them and there is no such thing as a bad one. This recipe is simple, but still filled with Tex-Mex flavor.

Ingredients:

2 green onions

2 cup shredded skinless rotisserie chicken meat

1 1/2 cups shredded Monterey Jack cheese

1 pickled jalapeño

1/4 cup fresh cilantro leaves

4 burrito-size flour tortillas

1/2 cup reduced-fat sour cream

Directions:

1. Start by preheating the toaster oven to 425 degrees.
2. Thinly slice the green onions and break apart.
3. Mix together chicken, cheese, jalapeno, and onions in a bowl then evenly divide the mixture onto one half of each tortilla.
4. Fold each half over the mixture and place each quesadilla onto a backing sheet.
5. Bake for 10 minutes.
6. Cut in half or quarters and serve with sour cream.

Nutritional Info: Calories: 830, Sodium: 921 mg, Dietary Fiber: 1.8 g, Total Fat: 59.0 g, Total Carbs: 13.8 g, Protein: 60.8 g.

Toaster Oven Chicken Paillard

Servings: 1 | Prep Time: 5 Minutes | Cook Time: 12 Minutes

This style of cooking is not as popular as it once was, but this is an awesome way to cook a tasty meal for one in just a few minutes.

Ingredients:

1/4 cup olive oil

1 boneless skinless chicken breast

Salt and pepper

1 garlic clove, sliced thin

1 small diced roma tomato

1/2 shaved fennel bulb

1/4 cup sliced mushroom

2 tablespoons sliced black olives

1 1/2 teaspoons capers

2 sprigs fresh thyme

1 tablespoon chopped fresh parsley

Directions:

1. Start by pounding the chicken down until it is about 1/2 inch thick.

2. Preheat the toaster oven to 400 degrees and brush the bottom of a baking pan with olive oil.

3. Sprinkle salt and pepper on both sides of the chicken and place it in the baking pan.

4. In a bowl, mix together all the other ingredients including the rest of the olive oil.

5. Spoon the mix over the chicken and bake for 12 minutes.

Nutritional Info: Calories: 797, Sodium: 471 mg, Dietary Fiber: 6.0 g, Total Fat: 63.7 g, Total Carbs: 16.4 g, Protein: 45.8 g.

Toaster Oven Fish and Chips

Servings: 4 | Prep Time: 40 Minutes | Cook Time: 17 Minutes

People all around the world love themselves some fish and chips, something that is so bland, yet one of the more exotic foods in the English stable. This recipe is not bland, but it does stay true to the English tradition.

Ingredients:

1 3/4 pounds potatoes

4 tablespoons olive oil

1 1/4 teaspoons kosher salt

1 1/4 teaspoons black pepper

8 sprigs fresh thyme

4 (6-ounce) pieces cod

1 lemon

1 clove garlic

2 tablespoons capers

Directions:

1. Start by preheating your Black and Decker toaster oven to 450 degrees.

2. Cut the potatoes into 1 inch chunks.

3. Combine potatoes, 2 tablespoons oil, salt, and thyme in a baking tray and toss.

4. Thin into a flat layer and bake for 30 minutes.

5. Wrap the mixture in foil to keep warm.

6. Wipe the tray with a paper towel and then lay the cod in the tray.

7. Slice the lemon and top the cod with lemon, salt, pepper, and thyme.

8. Drizzle the rest of the oil over the cod and bake for 12 minutes.

9. Place the cod and potatoes on separate plates and bake together for an additional 5 minutes.

10. Combine and serve.

Nutritional Info: Calories: 442, Sodium: 1002 mg, Dietary Fiber: 5.4 g, Total Fat: 15.8 g, Total Carbs: 32.7 g, Protein: 42.5 g.

Toaster Oven Pizza Bagels

Servings: 4 | Prep Time: 5 Minutes | Cook Time: 10 Minutes

Pizza bagels are just awesome no matter what time of day it is. This particular recipe dresses up the pizza bagel to give it a little adult flair.

Ingredients:

2 whole wheat bagels

1/4 cup marinara sauce

1/4 teaspoon Italian seasoning

1/8 teaspoon red pepper flakes

3/4 cups shredded low-moisture mozzarella cheese

1/4 cup chopped green pepper

3 tablespoons sliced black olives

Fresh basil

1 teaspoon parmesan cheese

Directions:

1. Start by preheating your toaster oven to 375 degrees and line a pan with parchment paper.

2. Cut the bagels in half and lay on the pan with inside facing up. Spread sauce over each half.

3. Sprinkle red pepper over each half. Sprinkle 2 tablespoons of mozzarella over each half.

4. Top each half with olives and peppers, then top with another tablespoon of mozzarella.

5. Bake for 8 minutes, then switch to broil and broil for another 2 minutes. Top with basil and parmesan and serve.

Nutritional Info: Calories: 222, Sodium: 493 mg, Dietary Fiber: 1.9 g, Total Fat: 6.1 g, Total Carbs: 30.2 g, Protein: 12.1 g.

Tuna Melt

Servings: 1 | Prep Time: 5 Minutes | Cook Time: 7 Minutes

No matter what time of day it is, nothing beats a classic tuna melt. This recipe has just enough to make the ordinary extraordinary without having to put in too much work.

Ingredients:

1 (6-ounce) can tuna, drained and flaked

2 tablespoons mayonnaise

1 pinch salt

1 teaspoon balsamic vinegar

1 teaspoon Dijon mustard

2 slices whole wheat bread

2 teaspoons chopped dill pickle

1/4 cup shredded sharp cheddar cheese

Directions:

1. Start by preheating your toaster oven to 375 degrees.

2. Put your bread in in the toaster while it warms.

3. Mix together tuna, mayo, salt, vinegar, mustard, and pickle in a small bowl.

4. Remove the bread from the oven and put the tuna mix on one side and the cheese on the other.

5. Return to toaster oven and bake for 7 minutes.

6. Combine slices, cut, and serve.

Nutritional Info: Calories: 688, Sodium: 1024 mg, Dietary Fiber: 4.1 g, Total Fat: 35.0 g, Total Carbs: 31.0 g, Protein: 59.9 g.

Turkey Chimichangas

Servings: 4 | Prep Time: 10 Minutes | Cook Time: 15 Minutes

Chimichangas are a highly underrated Mexican food that keeps my family happy weekly. When you make them with turkey it makes them a healthier option for the family.

Ingredients:

1 pound thickly sliced smoked turkey from deli counter, chopped

1 tablespoon chili powder

2 cups shredded slaw cabbage

1 to 2 chipotles in adobo sauce

1 cup tomato sauce

3 chopped scallions

Salt and pepper

4 (12-inch) flour tortillas

1 1/2 cups pepper jack cheese

2 tablespoons olive oil

1 cup sour cream

2 tablespoons chopped cilantro

Directions:

1. Start by preheating toaster oven to 400 degrees.
2. In a medium bowl mix together turkey and chili powder.
3. Add cabbage, chipotles, tomato sauce, and scallions; mix well.
4. Season mix with salt and pepper and turn a few times.
5. Warm tortillas in a microwave or on a flat top.
6. Lay cheese flat in each tortilla and top with turkey mix.
7. Fold in top and bottom, then roll to close.
8. Brush the baking tray will oil then place chimichangas on tray and brush each of them with oil.

9. Bake for 15 minutes or until tortilla is golden brown.

10. Top with sour cream and cilantro and serve.

Nutritional Info: Calories: 638, Sodium: 1785 mg, Dietary Fiber: 4.2 g, Total Fat: 44.0 g, Total Carbs: 23.9 g, Protein: 38.4 g.

10

Sides

Avocado Tomato Grape Salad with Crunchy Potato Croutons

Servings: 2 | Prep Time: 1 Hour 35 Minutes | Cook Time: 10 Minutes

There is a lot that goes into this recipe, so it takes some planning, but the end result is sure to be a crowd favorite.

Ingredients:

Potato croutons:

1 medium-small russet potato

2 cloves garlic

1 tablespoon extra light olive oil

1 tablespoon nutritional yeast

1/2 teaspoon garlic powder

1/2 teaspoon onion powder

1/2 teaspoon dried thyme

1/2 teaspoon dried rosemary

1/2 teaspoon dried oregano

1/2 teaspoon chili powder

1/4 teaspoon himalayan/sea salt

1/3 teaspoon cayenne pepper

A pinch red pepper flakes

Black pepper to taste

Salad:

1 cup grape tomatoes

A small handful dried cranberries

A small handful green grapes

2-3 sprigs cilantro

1 avocado

2 tablespoons extra virgin olive oil

1 tablespoon nutritional yeast

1 tablespoon lemon juice

1/2 teaspoon pure maple syrup

1/4 teaspoon salt

A few sprinkles ground pepper

A small handful toasted pecans

Directions:

1. Peel and cut potatoes into 1 inch cubes.

2. Place potatoes in water for an hour with a pinch of salt.

3. When the hour is up, preheat the toaster oven to 450 degrees.

4. Drain the potatoes and dry them on multiple layers of paper towels, then return them to the bowl.

5. Peel and mince the garlic, then add it to the bowl.

6. Add the rest of the crouton ingredients to the bowl and stir together.

7. Lay potatoes across a greased baking sheet in a single layer and bake for 35 minutes, flipping half way through.

8. Combine oil, yeast, syrup, lemon juice, salt and pepper together to create your salad dressing.

9. Slice the tomatoes in half and put in a bowl with cranberries and grapes.

10. Chop cilantro and add to bowl. Scoop out avocado and cut it into smaller pieces and add to bowl.

11. Drizzle in dressing and mix well. Add potatoes and mix again, top with pecans and serve.

Nutritional Info: Calories: 1032, Sodium: 560 mg, Dietary Fiber: 22.8 g, Total Fat: 84.9 g, Total Carbs: 64.2 g, Protein: 17.0 g.

Baked Parmesan Zucchini

Servings: 4 | Prep Time: 10 Minutes | Cook Time: 20 Minutes

Zucchini is an awesome alternative to less healthy sides; this recipe is so delicious that you may forget about those other sides all together.

Ingredients:

4 zucchinis

1/2 cup grated parmesan

1/2 teaspoon dried thyme

1/2 teaspoon dried oregano

1/2 teaspoon dried basil

1/4 teaspoon garlic powder

Salt and pepper to taste

2 tablespoons olive oil

2 tablespoons chopped fresh parsley leaves

Directions:

1. Start by preheating the toaster oven to 350 degrees.
2. Quarter the zucchini lengthwise.
3. Mix together parmesan, dried herbs, garlic powder, salt, and pepper.
4. Lay the zucchini flat on a greased pan and drizzle with olive oil.
5. Pour the parmesan mix over the zucchini.
6. Bake at 350 for 15 minutes then switch the setting to broil for another 3 minutes.

Nutritional Info: Calories: 189, Sodium: 295 mg, Dietary Fiber: 2.4 g, Total Fat: 13.7 g, Total Carbs: 8.1 g, Protein: 12.0 g.

Garlic Bread Bites

Servings: 12 | Prep Time: 10 Minutes | Cook Time: 7 Minutes

I wouldn't trust someone who said they don't like garlic bread. These bites are a great side dish to pair with many courses, I would suggest pizza or spaghetti.

Ingredients:

2 ciabatta loaves

1 stick butter at room temperature

4-6 crushed garlic cloves

Chopped parsley

2 tablespoons finely grated parmesan

Directions:

1. Start by cutting the bread in half and toasting it crust side down for 2 minutes.

2. Mix the butter, garlic, and parsley together and spread over the bread.

3. Sprinkle parmesan over the bread and toast in your Black and Decker toaster oven for another 5 minutes.

Nutritional Info: Calories: 191, Sodium: 382 mg, Dietary Fiber: 1.0 g, Total Fat: 9.4 g, Total Carbs: 21.7 g, Protein: 4.9 g.

Garlic Fries

Servings: 1 | Prep Time: 10 Minutes | Cook Time: 30 Minutes

Regular old fries can get pretty boring so it always helps to spice them up a bit. This recipe takes fries from a side to go with chicken nuggets to a side to go with a nice porterhouse.

Ingredients:

Roasted Garlic:

1 small head of garlic	*2 teaspoons olive oil*

Baked Fries:

2 medium Potatoes	*Salt*
2 teaspoons olive oil	*Pepper*

Garlic Fries Topping:

1/4 cup minced parsley	*1/8 teaspoon salt*
1 teaspoon olive oil	*2 cloves of roasted garlic*

Directions:

1. Start by preheating the toaster oven to 425 degrees and lining a baking sheet with parchment paper.

2. Remove the outer layer from the garlic and chop off the top.

3. Drizzle oil over the garlic filling the top.

4. Cut your potatoes into fries and toss with oil, salt, and pepper.

5. Lay in a single layer on a greased baking sheet and a garlic head, bake for 30 minutes turning fries half way through.

6.   Remove two cloves of the garlic head and mince both cloves and parsley.

7.   Stir the garlic mix in olive oil and salt.

8.   Drizzle over fries and serve.

Nutritional Info: Calories: 513, Sodium: 326 mg, Dietary Fiber: 10.9 g, Total Fat: 23.9 g, Total Carbs: 70.8 g, Protein: 8.2 g.

Green Mango Salad

Servings: 6 | Prep Time: 10 Minutes | Cook Time: 10 Minutes

Be careful with this side salad, it is so good that it might make the main dish jealous.

Ingredients:

1/3 cup chopped cashew

2 mangoes

1/3 cup chopped fresh coriander

1/3 cup chopped mint

2 tablespoons lime juice

4 teaspoons sugar

4 teaspoons fish sauce

1 tablespoon olive oil

1/4 teaspoon asian chili sauce

1/4 teaspoon hot pepper sauce

1 sweet red pepper thinly sliced

1 cup thinly sliced red onion

Directions:

1. Start by toasting the cashews in your toaster oven for 8 minutes.

2. Cut pointed ends off of mangoes, then skin.

3. Cut the mangoes into lengthwise into thin slices, then stack them on top of each other and cut again into thin strips.

4. In a large bowl, mix together mint, coriander, lime juice, fish sauce, sugar, olive oil, and chili sauce.

5. Add mangoes, red pepper, and onions to the bowl and toss.

6. Transfer salad to plates and sprinkle with cashews before serving.

Nutritional Info: Calories: 140, Sodium: 317 mg, Dietary Fiber: 2.7 g, Total Fat: 6.2 g, Total Carbs: 20.7 g, Protein: 2.3 g.

Honey-Roasted Carrots with Sesame Seeds

Servings: 4 | Prep Time: 5 Minutes | Cook Time: 10 Minutes

Never thought that carrots could actually be an exciting side dish? This recipe takes carrots to a gourmet level in a simple way.

Ingredients:

2 bunches baby carrots

2 tablespoons olive oil

2 tablespoons honey

Salt and pepper to taste

1 tablespoon soy sauce

1 tablespoon chopped fresh parsley

2 teaspoons sesame seeds

Directions:

1. Start by preheating the toaster oven to 450 degrees.
2. Line a pan with parchment paper and put in the oven while it heats.
3. In a small bowl, mix together oil and 1 tablespoon honey.
4. Remove carrots from oven and drizzle honey mix over carrots.
5. Sprinkle with salt and pepper.
6. Roast carrots for 10 minutes.
7. Mix soy sauce and remaining honey together and toss in carrots.
8. Sprinkle parsley and sesame seeds over the carrots and serve.

Nutritional Info: Calories: 142, Sodium: 314 mg, Dietary Fiber: 3.5 g, Total Fat: 7.9 g, Total Carbs: 18.7 g, Protein: 1.3 g.

Lemon-Garlic Kale Salad

Servings: 8 | Prep Time: 10 Minutes | Cook Time: 10 Minutes

This is an awesome light salad to join a healthy protein like a grilled chicken breast or low-fat steak. It may be light, but it holds its own in the flavor department.

Ingredients:

2 cups sliced almonds

1/3 cup lemon juice

1 teaspoon salt

1 1/2 cups olive oil

4 cloves crushed garlic

12 ounces kale with stems removed

Directions:

1. Set your toaster oven to toast and toast almonds for about 5 minutes.

2. Combine lemon juice and salt in a small bowl then add olive oil and a garlic, mix well and set aside.

3. Cut kale into thin ribbons. Place the kale in a bowl and sprinkle with almonds.

4. Remove garlic from dressing then add desired amount of dressing to kale and toss.

5. Add dressing as necessary and serve.

Nutritional Info: Calories: 487, Sodium: 312 mg, Dietary Fiber: 3.7 g, Total Fat: 49.8 g, Total Carbs: 10.2 g, Protein: 6.5 g.

Lemon-Thyme Bruschetta

Servings: 10 | Prep Time: 5 Minutes | Cook Time: 7 Minutes

This is great for a side, appetizer, or snack. It is easy to whip together and doesn't take a whole lot of time either.

Ingredients:

1 baguette

8 ounces ricotta cheese

1 lemon

Salt

Freshly cracked black pepper

Honey

8 sprigs fresh thyme

Directions:

1. Start by preheating the toaster oven to 425 degrees.

2. Thinly slice the baguette and zest lemon.

3. Mix ricotta and lemon zest together and season with salt and pepper.

4. Toast the baguette slices for 7 minutes or until they start to brown.

5. Spread ricotta mix over slices.

6. Drizzle with and top with thyme, then serve.

Nutritional Info: Calories: 60, Sodium: 71 mg, Dietary Fiber: 0.6 g, Total Fat: 2.0 g, Total Carbs: 7.6 g, Protein: 3.5 g.

Oven Roasted Asparagus

Servings: 4 | Prep Time: 2 Minutes | Cook Time: 10 Minutes

Asparagus is an awesome side and a sadly overlooked vegetable in many cases. This simple recipe showcases the brilliance of asparagus.

Ingredients:

1 bunch asparagus

4 tablespoons olive oil

Salt and pepper to taste

Directions:

1. Start by pre-heating the toaster oven to 425.
2. Wash the asparagus and cut off the bottom inch.
3. Toss the asparagus in olive oil and lay flat on a baking sheet.
4. Sprinkle salt and pepper over asparagus.
5. Roast in the oven for 10 minutes.

Nutritional Info: Calories: 127, Sodium: 1 mg, Dietary Fiber: 0.7 g, Total Fat: 14.0 g, Total Carbs: 1.3 g, Protein: 0.7 g.

Roasted Beets with Grapefruit Glaze

Servings: 5 | Prep Time: 50 Minutes | Cook Time: 10 Minutes

Beets are one of the more unique side dishes out there because of their undeniable flavor and sweetness. The sweetness is accented even more when we top the beats with a grapefruit vinaigrette.

Ingredients:

3 pounds beets

1 cup fresh-squeezed grapefruit juice (this took 2 medium grapefruits for me)

1 tablespoon rice vinegar

3 scant tablespoons pure maple syrup

1 tablespoon corn starch

Directions:

1. Start by preheating your toaster oven to 450 degrees. Place beats in a roasting pan and sprinkle them with water.

2. Roast beets until they are soft enough to be pierced with a fork, this should be at least 40 minutes.

3. Remove beats and let them cool until you can handle them.

4. Peel skin off the beets and slice them into thin slices.

5. Mix together the grapefruit juice, syrup, and vinegar in a small bowl.

6. Pour cornstarch into a medium sauce pan and slowly add grapefruit mix. Stir together until there are no clumps.

7. Heat the sauce to a light boil then reduce heat and simmer for 5 minutes, stirring often.

8. Drizzle the glaze over the beets and serve.

Nutritional Info: Calories: 175, Sodium: 211 mg, Dietary Fiber: 6.0 g, Total Fat: 0.6 g, Total Carbs: 40.7 g, Protein: 4.9 g.

Roasted Brussels Sprouts

Servings: 6 | Prep Time: 5 Minutes | Cook Time: 30 Minutes

I have heard tale that Brussels sprouts are kind of hard to get kids to eat. This simple recipe goes miles to improve the taste and texture of the pungent vegetable.

Ingredients:

1 1/2 pounds brussels sprouts, ends trimmed and yellow leaves removed

3 tablespoons olive oil

1 teaspoon salt

1/2 teaspoon black pepper

Directions:

1. Start by preheating the toaster oven to 400 degrees.

2. Toss Brussels sprouts in a large bowl, drizzle with olive oil, sprinkle with salt and pepper then toss.

3. Roast for 30 minutes.

Nutritional Info: Calories: 109, Sodium: 416 mg, Dietary Fiber: 4.3 g, Total Fat: 7.4 g, Total Carbs: 10.4 g, Protein: 3.9 g.

Roasted Curried Cauliflower

Servings: 4 | Prep Time: 10 Minutes | Cook Time: 35 Minutes

I like cauliflower, but it can be a little bland sometimes. This recipe helps a cauliflower out by dressing it up a little bit.

Ingredients:

1 1/2 tablespoons extra-virgin olive oil

1 teaspoon mustard seeds

1 teaspoon cumin seeds

3/4 teaspoon curry powder

3/4 teaspoon coarse salt

1 large head cauliflower

Olive oil cooking spray

Directions:

1. Start by preheating the toaster oven to 375 degrees.
2. Mix together curry, mustard, cumin, and salt in a large bowl.
3. Break the cauliflower into pieces and add it to the bowl.
4. Toss the bowl until the cauliflower is completely covered in the spice mix.
5. Coat a baking sheet in olive oil spray and lay the cauliflower in a single layer over the sheet.
6. Roast for 35 minutes.

Nutritional Info: Calories: 105, Sodium: 64 mg, Dietary Fiber: 5.6 g, Total Fat: 5.9 g, Total Carbs: 11.9 g, Protein: 4.5 g.

Roasted Potatoes

Servings: 4 | Prep Time: 5 Minutes | Cook Time: 25 minutes

Potatoes are the perfect food for sides because they can be used in so many ways. These roasted potatoes are a great alternative to dull French fries or time consuming baked potatoes.

Ingredients:

1 small bag baby or fingerling potatoes

3 tablespoons olive oil

Salt and pepper to taste

2 teaspoons rosemary

2 teaspoons thyme

Directions:

1. Start by preheating the toaster oven to 400 degrees.
2. Toss potatoes in olive oil and put them on a baking sheet.
3. Pierce each potato to prevent from overexpansion.
4. Sprinkle salt, pepper, rosemary, and thyme over the potatoes.
5. Roast for 25 minutes.

Nutritional Info: Calories: 123, Sodium: 3 mg, Dietary Fiber: 1.2 g, Total Fat: 10.7 g, Total Carbs: 7.5 g, Protein: 0.9 g.

Roasted Radishes with Brown Butter, Lemon, and Radish Tops

Servings: 4 | Prep Time: 15 Minutes | Cook Time: 20 Minutes

I tend to embrace the spicier side of life so it is no surprise that radishes are one of my favorite vegetables. This recipe takes something that is already great and makes it just a little better.

Ingredients:

2 bunches medium radishes

1 1/2 tablespoons olive oil

Coarse kosher salt

2 tablespoons (1/4 stick) unsalted butter

1 teaspoon fresh lemon juice

Directions:

1. Start by preheating the toaster oven to 450 degrees.

2. Cut tops off of radishes (about 1/2-inch) and coarsely chop them and set aside.

3. Cut radishes down the middle lengthwise and place in a large bowl.

4. Add olive oil to the bowl and toss to coat. Place the radishes flat side down and sprinkle with salt. Roast radishes for 20 minutes.

5. Towards the end of the roasting time, melt the butter in a small sauce pan until it browns and add lemon juice.

6. Transfer the radishes to a serving bowl and drizzle with butter, sprinkle with chopped radish tops and serve.

Nutritional Info: Calories: 96, Sodium: 42 mg, Dietary Fiber: 0 g, Total Fat: 11.0 g, Total Carbs: 0.1 g, Protein: 0.1 g.

Roasted Spring Vegetables

Servings: 4 | Prep Time: 10 Minutes | Cook Time: 20 Minutes

This is a great way to welcome in spring and add some variety to the dinner table.

Ingredients:

1 pound assorted spring vegetables (such as carrots, asparagus, radishes, spring onions, or sugar snap peas)

4 unpeeled garlic cloves

2 tablespoons olive oil

Salt and pepper to taste

Directions:

1. Start by preheating the toaster oven to 450 degrees.
2. Combines vegetables, garlic, oil, salt, and pepper in a bowl and toss.
3. Roast for 20 minutes or until the vegetables start to brown.

Nutritional Info: Calories: 105, Sodium: 255 mg, Dietary Fiber: 4.4 g, Total Fat: 7.3 g, Total Carbs: 9.1 g, Protein: 1.8 g.

Roasted Tomatoes and Garlic

Servings: 4 | Prep Time: 5 Minutes | Cook Time 45 Minutes

Tomatoes are actually a lot like potatoes in the fact that they can be prepared as sides in many different ways. This is just one of the many delicious, and healthy, ways you can use to prepare tomatoes as a side.

Ingredients:

10 medium sized tomatoes

10 garlic cloves

bread crumbs

Thyme

Sage

Oregano

Directions:

1. Start by finely chopping garlic and herbs.
2. Cut tomatoes in half and place on a baking sheet lined with parchment paper.
3. Pour garlic and herb mixture over tomatoes.
4. Using your Black and Decker toaster oven, roast at 350 degrees for 30 minutes.
5. Top with bread crumbs and roast for another 15 minutes.

Nutritional Info: Calories: 103, Sodium: 68 mg, Dietary Fiber: 5.4 g, Total Fat: 1.3 g, Total Carbs: 21.4 g, Protein: 4.4 g.

Roasted Vegetable and Kale Salad

Servings: 4 | Prep Time: 10 Minutes | Cook Time: 40 Minutes

This is an awesome light side that can be paired with so many dishes. It could also serve as an appetizer or you could double the recipe and add some chicken for a main course.

Ingredients:

1 bunch kale stems removed and chopped into ribbons

4 small or 2 large beets, peeled and cut roughly into 1-inch pieces

1/2 small butternut squash, peeled and cubed into 1 inch pieces

1 small red onion, sliced into 8 wedges

1 medium fennel bulb, sliced into 8 wedges

1 red pepper

3 tablespoons olive oil

1/2 cup coarsely chopped walnuts

3/4 teaspoons salt

pepper to taste

2 ounces goat cheese

Directions:

1. Cut the beets and pepper into one inch pieces.

2. Remove the stems from the kale and chop into thin pieces.

3. Cut fennel and red onion into wedges.

4. Preheat the toaster oven to 425 degrees.

5. Toss together all vegetables, except for kale, in a large bowl with oil, salt, and pepper.

6. Spread over a baking sheet and roast for 40 minutes turning halfway through.

7. At the 30-minute mark, remove the tray and sprinkle walnuts over and around the vegetables.

8. Toss the kale in your desired dressing and top with vegetables. Crumble goat cheese over the salad and serve.

Nutritional Info: Calories: 321, Sodium: 569 mg, Dietary Fiber: 5.5 g, Total Fat: 25.1 g, Total Carbs: 17.5 g, Protein: 11.1 g.

Spanakopita

This traditional Greek dish works great as a heavy side or even an appetizer. It will stand out at your next get together and garner you some kitchen recognition.

Ingredients:

- 3 tablespoons olive oil
- 2-1/2 pounds spinach
- 1 large onion
- 1 bunch green onions
- 2 cloves garlic
- 1/2 cup chopped fresh parsley
- 1/4 cup fresh dill
- 1/4 teaspoon ground nutmeg
- 2 eggs
- 1/2 cup ricotta cheese
- 1 cup crumbled feta cheese
- 3/4 teaspoons salt
- 1/2 teaspoon pepper
- 16 sheets of thawed phyllo dough
- 1/4 cup olive oil

Directions:

1. Start by chopping all of your vegetables into fine pieces.
2. Preheat the toaster oven to 350 degrees.
3. Put the olive oil in a large skillet and heat it over medium heat.
4. Sauté both onions and garlic until garlic starts to brown.
5. Add spinach, parsley, dill, and nutmeg and stir until spinach begins to wilt.
6. Break eggs in medium bowl and mix in ricotta, feta, salt, and pepper.
7. Add spinach mix to egg mix and stir until combined.

8.   Lay a sheet of phyllo dough on a baking sheet (it should overlap the edges) and brush with oil, repeat this process 7 more times.

9.   Spread the spinach mix over the dough and fold the overlapping edges in.

10.   Brush the edges with olive oil. Add remaining dough one sheet at a time, brushing with oil as you go.

11.   Tuck the overlapping edges down to seal the filling in the dough.

12.   Bake for 40 Minutes or until lightly browned.

Nutritional Info: Calories: 458, Sodium: 991 mg, Dietary Fiber: 5.8 g, Total Fat: 27.7 g, Total Carbs: 39.8 g, Protein: 16.9 g.

11

Snacks

Baked Avocados with Strawberry Salsa

Servings: 3 | Prep Time: 10 Minutes | Cook Time: 10 Minutes

This recipe just screams spring and it is a great, light, healthy, snack to enjoy on your back porch.

Ingredients:

3 avocados

Olive oil

1 cup strawberries

2 scallions

2 tablespoons goat cheese crumbles

2 tablespoons fresh basil

1 tablespoon balsamic vinegar

Directions:

1. Start by stemming and quartering the strawberries and thinly slicing the basil and scallions.

2. Preheat the toaster oven to 400 degrees.

3. Cut the avocados in half lengthwise and remove the pit.

4. Lay the avocados on a baking sheet flesh side up and brush with olive oil.

5. Bake avocados for 8 minutes.

6. While the avocados bake mix together all the other ingredients in a medium bowl.

7. Add strawberry salsa to each avocado slice and return to the oven for another 3 minutes.

8. Serve warm.

Nutritional Info: Calories: 474, Sodium: 173 mg, Dietary Fiber: 60 g, Total Fat: 42.9 g, Total Carbs: 22.1 g, Protein: 7.3 g.

Baked Eggs with Marinara and Parmesan

Servings: 4 | Prep Time: 10 Minutes | Cook Time: 15 Minutes

This recipe is simple, unique, and perfect for when you want to take even snack time to a gourmet level.

Ingredients:

8 eggs

1 cup marinara sauce

1/4 cup whipping cream

1/4 cup parmesan cheese

Salt and pepper

Chives for garnish

Directions:

1. Start by greasing 4 ramekins.
2. Preheat the toaster oven to 400 degrees.
3. Pour 1/4 cup of marinara into each ramekin.
4. Crack 2 eggs into each ramekin.
5. Stop eggs with 1 tablespoon each of whipping cream and parmesan.
6. Sprinkle with salt and pepper and bake for 15 minutes.
7. While the eggs bake chop your chives.
8. Remove from oven, top with chives, and serve with toast.

Nutritional Info: Calories: 250, Sodium: 519 mg, Dietary Fiber: 1.6 g, Total Fat: 15.9 g, Total Carbs: 10.0 g, Protein: 17.1 g.

Bread Pudding

Servings: 12 | Prep Time: 10 Minutes | Cook Time: 40 Minutes

Bread pudding is a treat in my house and this is my favorite recipe because it is relatively quick and easy.

Ingredients:

1 loaf bread

2 cup evaporated milk

1 cup condensed milk

1 cup raisins

Directions:

1. Start by preheating the toaster oven to 400 degrees.
2. Pour evaporated milk into pan.
3. Add bread and mash together with hands.
4. Add condensed milk.
5. Add in raisins and stir.
6. Bake for 40 minutes, then allow to cool before cutting.

Nutritional Info: Calories: 329, Sodium: 475 mg, Dietary Fiber: 1.8 g, Total Fat: 7.4 g, Total Carbs: 57.2 g, Protein: 9.7 g.

Coconut Twice Baked Sweet Potato

Servings: 8 | Prep Time: 30 Minutes | Cook Time: 20 Minutes

This one is so decadent that it almost belongs under deserts. It is a great way to get the family to eat sweet potatoes.

Ingredients:

4 medium sweet potatoes

1/2 cup coconut milk

1 tablespoon maple syrup

1 teaspoon minced fresh gingerroot

1 teaspoon adobo sauce

1/2 teaspoon salt

1/4 cup chopped pecans

1/4 cup flaked coconut

Directions:

1. Scrub the sweet potatoes and pierce with a fork, microwave for 10 minutes.

2. Cut each potato down the center lengthwise and scoop out the inside into a bowl, keep the shells.

3. Preheat the toaster oven to 350 degrees. Mash the pulp with coconut milk, then stir in the adobo, salt, syrup, and ginger.

4. Spoon the mix back into the shells.

5. Place on a baking sheet and top with pecans and coconut.

6. Bake for 25 minutes.

Nutritional Info: Calories: 185, Sodium: 173 mg, Dietary Fiber: 3.2 g, Total Fat: 15.2 g, Total Carbs: 12.4 g, Protein: 2.4 g.

Lasagna Toasts

Servings: 4 | Prep Time: 15 Minutes | Cook Time: 10 Minutes

Hold onto your seats, because this one is going to blow you away. This incredible dish could really be used for anytime, but it makes for a ridiculously awesome snack or appetizer.

Ingredients:

4 slices Italian bread

1 medium zucchini

1 clove garlic

1 tablespoon olive oil

4 ripe plum tomatoes

Salt and pepper to taste

1 cup ricotta cheese

1/4 cup freshly grated romano cheese

4 ounces fresh mozzarella cheese

Directions:

1. Start by preheating the toaster oven to 450 degrees. Toast bread for 10 minutes.

2. Combine oil, garlic, and zucchini in a microwave safe bowl. Microwave on high for 4 minutes.

3. Add tomatoes, salt, and pepper to the bowl and microwave for another 3 minutes.

4. In a separate bowl mix together ricotta and romano with salt and pepper.

5. Spread ricotta mixture on each bread slice, then top with tomato mixture.

6. Place mozzarella over each slice and place on a baking sheet.

7. Bake for 10 minutes.

Nutritional Info: Calories: 318, Sodium: 506 mg, Dietary Fiber: 2.2 g, Total Fat: 18.1 g, Total Carbs: 17.9 g, Protein: 22.9 g.

Mushroom Strudel

Servings: 4 – 6 | Prep Time: 20 Minutes | Cook Time: 15 Minutes

Mushroom and strudel are two foods that don't sound like they would every go together. They work in a weird way here that is actually quite delectable.

Ingredients:

12 sheets phyllo

3 tablespoons olive oil

1 egg

1 pound mushrooms

1 medium onion

3 tablespoons butter

1 tablespoon dry sherry

1 tablespoon all-purpose flour

Leaves from 1 sprig of thyme

6 tablespoons freshly grated parmesan

Salt and pepper to taste

Directions:

1. Start by preheating the toaster oven to 400 degrees.

2. Line a baking sheet with parchment paper.

3. Pour the oil into a skillet on medium heat and sauté the mushrooms and onions for about 7 minutes.

4. Pour in the sherry and cook at medium heat for another 3 minutes.

5. Mix in the flour, thyme salt, and pepper and remove from heat.

6. Melt butter.

7. Remove one phyllo sheet and brush one half of the sheet lengthwise with butter.

8. Fold the unbuttered side over the buttered side and smooth out any wrinkles or bubbles.

9. Again, brush one half of the phyllo with butter, and fold the unbuttered side over it again. You'll end up with one long column.

10. Place one spoonful of mushroom filling at the end of the column and sprinkle parmesan on top.

11. Fold one corner of the phyllo over the filling to create a triangle shape and keep folding over triangles until you reach the other end of the column (it's like you are folding a flag).

12. Beat the egg and brush it over the strudel. Repeat for as many strudels as you can safely fit and bake for 15 minutes.

Nutritional Info: Calories: 312, Sodium: 376 mg, Dietary Fiber: 2.0 g, Total Fat: 19.2 g, Total Carbs: 25.9 g, Protein: 11.1 g.

Nacho Avocado Toast

Servings: 2 | Prep Time: 10 Minutes | Cook Time: 5 Minutes

I'm not sure if there are words to describe this vegan recipe. If all vegan meals were this good, I would probably consider going vegan.

Ingredients:

2 slices of whole grain bread

3 tablespoons black bean & cilantro spread

3 tablespoons guacamole

1/2 cup baby spinach

1/4 small red onion

1/4 cup frozen sweet corn

1/4 cup plant-based nacho cheese sauce

Directions:

1. Mince spinach and onion.
2. Put the corn in a strainer and run hot water over it for a minute to thaw.
3. Place the toast on a baking screen and spread with bean and cilantro spread.
4. Spread guacamole over the bean spread. Sprinkle spinach and onion over the top. Sprinkle corn over the top.
5. Toast with your toaster oven for 4 minutes or until the toast reaches your desired level of crispness.
6. While the bread toasts warm the cheese sauce in the microwave or in a heat safe bowl on top of the oven.
7. Drizzle sauce over toast and serve.

Nutritional Info: Calories: 117, Sodium: 221 mg, Dietary Fiber: 3.6 g, Total Fat: 4.2 g, Total Carbs: 18.8 g, Protein: 4.2 g.

Parmesan Hash Brown Cups

Servings: 6 | Prep Time: 10 Minutes | Cook Time: 75 Minutes

These are great for a delicious snack or a breakfast surprise. They are easy to throw together and I guarantee your family will be begging for these.

Ingredients:

1 (20-ounce) bag hash browns, shredded

3 green onions

1/2 cup grated parmesan cheese

1 teaspoon kosher salt

1/2 teaspoon black pepper

2 tablespoons olive oil

Directions:

1. Start by chopping up the green onions.

2. Preheat the toaster oven to 350 degrees.

3. Combine potatoes, cheese, onion, salt, and pepper in a large bowl.

4. Drizzle olive oil over the potato mix and toss with a fork.

5. Grease a muffin tin and spoon mixture into tin.

6. Pack the mixture into each cup by pushing it down with the rounded side of the spoon.

7. Bake for 75 minutes.

Nutritional Info: Calories: 325, Sodium: 805 mg, Dietary Fiber: 3.3 g, Total Fat: 18.7 g, Total Carbs: 34.2 g, Protein: 6.2 g.

Toaster Oven Garlic Kale Chips

Servings: 2 | Prep Time: 5 Minutes | Cook Time: 10 Minutes

I love kale chips, they are a great healthy alternative to regular potato chips, and just like potato chips you can have all kinds of flavors.

Ingredients:

4 cups kale

1 tablespoon olive oil

1/4 teaspoon pepper

1/4 teaspoon garlic powder

Salt to taste

Directions:

1. Start by preheating your toaster oven to 350 degrees.
2. Tear kale into one inch pieces and place in a bowl.
3. Add oil, pepper, garlic powder, and salt, and toss until kale is well coated.
4. Bake for 10 minutes.

Nutritional Info: Calories: 128, Sodium: 136 mg, Dietary Fiber: 2.1 g, Total Fat: 7.0 g, Total Carbs: 14.4 g, Protein: 4.1 g.

Toaster Oven Pita Chips

Servings: 1 | Prep Time: 5 Minutes | Cook Time: 8 Minutes

Pita chips are a delicious, healthier option to potato chips and great to pair with salsa or humus.

Ingredients:

1 regular whole wheat pita

1 teaspoon olive oil

Salt to taste

Directions:

1. Start by preheating your Black and Decker toaster oven at 375 degrees.

2. Brush both sides of the pita with oil and sprinkle with salt.

3. Cut pita into 6 wedges.

4. Place wedges on ungreased baking sheet and bake for 8 minutes.

Nutritional Info: Calories: 210, Sodium: 496 mg, Dietary Fiber: 4.7 g, Total Fat: 6.3 g, Total Carbs: 35.2 g, Protein: 6.3 g.

Tomato Grilled Cheese Bites

Servings: 1 | Prep Time: 2 Minutes | Cook Time: 2 Minutes

This is a great snack for any time and any occasion. It is not super healthy or incredibly unhealthy either; what it is a tasty snack that can be taken on the go.

Ingredients:

4 slices fresh tomato

2 whole grain crackers

1 ounce cheddar cheese

Salt to taste

Directions:

1. Start by preheating the broiler on high using your Black and
2. Decker toaster oven.
3. Place crackers on a cookie sheet.
4. Add tomato and sprinkle with salt.
5. Top with cheese and broil until cheese is fully melted.

Nutritional Info: Calories: 165, Sodium: 402 mg, Dietary Fiber: 0.8 g, Total Fat: 11.5 g, Total Carbs: 7.6 g, Protein: 8.2 g.

12

Deserts

Apple Tart

Servings: 1 | Prep Time: 10 Minutes | Cook Time: 15 Minutes

This is a simple recipe for a simple desert, sometimes the classics are the best.

Ingredients:

2 teaspoons light brown sugar

1/2 teaspoon ground cinnamon

1 (6-inch) flour tortilla

1 tablespoon unsalted butter

1/2 honey crisp apple

Salt to taste

Directions:

1. Melt butter and slice apples into 1/8-inch-thick slices.
2. Mix together cinnamon and sugar.
3. Brush tortilla with butter and sprinkle with half the sugar and cinnamon.
4. Toast in a toaster oven until tortilla crisps, about 3 minutes.
5. Arrange the apple slices in a circle around the tortilla.
6. Return to toaster oven and toast for another 10 minutes.
7. Sprinkle with salt to taste.

Nutritional Info: Calories: 227, Sodium: 250 mg, Dietary Fiber: 4.3 g, Total Fat: 12.4 g, Total Carbs: 30.1 g, Protein: 1.8 g.

Blackberry Peach Cobbler

Servings: 12 | Prep Time: 25 Minutes | Cook Time: 30 Minutes

This is another take on the classic cobbler. Mixing tart blackberries with sweet peach makes your tongue want to dance.

Ingredients:

1 1/2 cups sliced peaches

1 cup blackberries

3 tablespoons coconut sugar

1 1/2 teaspoons cinnamon

2 1/2 cups dry oats

1 egg

1/2 cup unsweetened applesauce

3/4 cups almond milk

1/2 cup chopped walnuts

1 tablespoon coconut oil, melted

1/2 teaspoon cinnamon

Directions:

1. Start by preheating the toaster oven to 350 degrees.
2. Combine peaches, berries, sugar, and 1 teaspoon cinnamon in a medium saucepan over medium heat. Simmer for about 20 minutes stirring regularly.
3. While the peaches cook, beat egg in a large bowl then mix in apple sauce and milk.
4. Put 2 cups oatmeal in a separate bowl and pour egg mixture over oatmeal.
5. Pour oatmeal into a greased baking pan and top with peach mixture.
6. Mix together coconut oil, walnuts, coconut sugar, and 1/2 teaspoon cinnamon, and pour over pan.
7. Bake for 30 Minutes

Nutritional Info: Calories: 176, Sodium: 9 mg, Dietary Fiber: 3.7 g, Total Fat: 9.4 g, Total Carbs: 20.6 g, Protein: 4.7 g.

Blueberry Croissant Puff

Servings: 10 | Prep Time: 30 Minutes | Cook Time: 40 Minutes

This is one of my favorite deserts, ever. It is so rich and creamy if it wasn't for my waistline I would probably eat every night.

Ingredients:

3 large croissants

1 cup fresh or frozen blueberries

1 package (8-ounce) cream cheese

2/3 cups sugar

2 eggs

1 teaspoon vanilla

1 cup milk

Directions:

1. Start by preheating toaster oven to 350 degrees.
2. Tear up croissants into 2 inch chunks and place them in a square pan.
3. Sprinkle blueberries over croissant chunks.
4. In a medium bowl, mix cream cheese, sugar, eggs, and vanilla.
5. Slowly add in milk mixing as you go.
6. Pour cream cheese mix over the croissants and let stand for 20 minutes.
7. Bake for 40 minutes.

Nutritional Info: Calories: 140, Sodium: 97 mg, Dietary Fiber: 0.5 g, Total Fat: 5.8 g, Total Carbs: 20.0 g, Protein: 3.2 g.

Oatmeal Cookie Peach Cobbler

Servings: 12 | Prep Time: 40 Minutes | Cook Time: 40 Minutes

This desert combines two favorites to create an entire new flavor profile. It is a fun and tasty desert that is perfect for a summertime get together.

Ingredients:

Topping:

1/2 cup granulated sugar

1/2 cup packed brown sugar

1/2 cup softened butter

2 teaspoons vanilla extract

1 large egg

1 cup all-purpose flour

1 cup old-fashioned rolled oats

1/2 teaspoon baking powder

1/2 teaspoon salt

Filling:

11 cups sliced peeled peaches

1/3 cup granulated sugar

2 tablespoons all-purpose flour

2 tablespoons fresh lemon juice

Directions:

1. Start by preheating your toaster oven to 350 degrees.
2. Combine butter and sugars in a medium bowl until creamed, set aside.
3. Add vanilla and egg and mix well.
4. Combine the flour, oats, and baking powder in a separate bowl.

5. Mix sugar mixture and flour mixture together.

6. Cover the bowl and refrigerate for half an hour.

7. While the topping chills make the filling by combining peaches, lemon juice, flour, and sugar in a bowl.

8. Spray a baking dish with cooking spray and fill it with peach mix.

9. Dollop spoonful of the topping evenly over the peaches. Bake for 40 minutes.

Nutritional Info: Calories: 281, Sodium: 160 mg, Dietary Fiber: 3.4 g, Total Fat: 9.0 g, Total Carbs: 48.5 g, Protein: 4.2 g.

Oatmeal Raisin Cookies

Servings: 12 | Prep Time: 10 Minutes | Cook Time: 20 Minutes

Is there a food in this universe that is more polarizing than oatmeal raisin cookies? This recipe may win over a few of those people who think they don't like oatmeal raisin.

Ingredients:

2 1/2 cups uncooked oatmeal

1 cup flour

2 eggs

1/2 teaspoon salt

1 cup butter

1 teaspoon vanilla

1 cup brown sugar

1/3 cup sugar

1 teaspoon baking soda

1 teaspoon ground cinnamon

1 cup raisins

Directions:

1. Start by preheating your toaster oven to 350 degrees.
2. Mix together vanilla, brown sugar, butter, and salt.
3. Add Sugar, eggs, baking soda, and cinnamon one at a time until fully mixed.
4. Stir in the oats, then stir in the raisins.
5. Drop spoonful of mixture onto an ungreased baking sheet (about six per batch).
6. Bake for 20 minutes.

Nutritional Info: Calories: 353, Sodium: 326 mg, Dietary Fiber: 2.6 g, Total Fat: 17.3 g, Total Carbs: 46.7 g, Protein: 4.8 g.

Peanut Butter and Jelly Bars

Servings: 8 | Prep Time: 10 Minutes | Cook Time: 20 Minutes

Some genius was sitting in their kitchen one day and thought to themselves, "How could I make peanut butter and jelly better?" Then they came up with an idea similar to this one.

Ingredients:

1/2 cup whole wheat pastry flour

1/2 teaspoon baking powder

1/4 teaspoon salt

1 small banana

1/4 cup smooth peanut butter

3 tablespoons real maple syrup

2 teaspoons melted coconut oil

1/2 teaspoon pure vanilla extract

2 tablespoons chopped raw shelled peanuts

2 tablespoons raspberry preserves

Directions:

1. Start by preheating the toaster oven to 350 degrees.
2. Mash banana.
3. Mix banana, syrup, oil, peanut butter, and vanilla in a bowl until thoroughly combined.
4. Add flour, salt, and baking powder to a large bowl and combine using a fork.
5. Create a hole in the flour mix and pour in banana mix.
6. Sprinkle with nuts and stir for 2 minutes.
7. Pour batter into a bread loaf pan lined with parchment paper. Drop 1/2 teaspoon drops of raspberry preserves over batter.

8.   Bake for 20 minutes.

9.   Allow to cool, then transfer using parchment paper to cut.

Nutritional Info: Calories: 143, Sodium: 78 mg, Dietary Fiber: 1.8 g, Total Fat: 6.5 g, Total Carbs: 19.0 g, Protein: 3.5 g.

Pear Crisp

Servings: 1 | Prep Time: 10 Minutes | Cook Time: 25 Minutes

Everyone loves how delicious apple crisp is, and I can't argue that, but it's been done. By replacing the apples with pears you get a whole new flavor profile that livens up a classic.

Ingredients:

1 cup pears

2 tablespoons rolled oats.

1 tablespoon whole wheat pastry flour

1 tablespoon brown sugar

1 tablespoon butter

1/2 teaspoon cinnamon

Fresh grated nutmeg to taste

Directions:

1. Start by peeling and slicing the pear into thin slices, about 1 cup.
2. Preheat the toaster oven to 375 degrees.
3. Place the pears in an oven safe dishes.
4. In a separate bowl, mix together all other ingredients and pour on top of pears.
5. Bake for 25 minutes.

Nutritional Info: Calories: 300, Sodium: 87 mg, Dietary Fiber: 7.4 g, Total Fat: 12.7 g, Total Carbs: 46.9 g, Protein: 2.9 g.

Plum Clafoutis

Servings: 8 | Prep Time: 10 Minutes | Cook Time: 45 Minutes

Some say it is a cobbler, others a custard, no matter what you call it, it is 100% delicious.

Ingredients:

2 tablespoons unsalted butter

1 cup whole milk

1/3 cup granulated sugar

1/2 teaspoon grated nutmeg

1/4 teaspoon salt

3 eggs

1/2 cup whole wheat pastry flour

4 plums

Directions:

1. Start by halving the plums and removing the pits.
2. Preheat the toaster oven to 400 degrees.
3. Melt butter in a large bowl and add in milk, sugar, nutmeg, salt, and eggs.
4. Spray an 8-inch square baking sheet and pour batter in the pan.
5. Push plums, inside down into the pan and bake for 45 minutes.

Nutritional Info: Calories: 137, Sodium: 129 mg, Dietary Fiber: 1.1 g, Total Fat: 5.7 g, Total Carbs: 17.9 g, Protein: 4.0 g.

Single Serving Chocolate Chip Cookies

Servings: 1 | Prep Time: 10 Minutes | Cook Time: 8 Minutes

Okay, so this one really doesn't need an explanation. If you don't love chocolate chip cookies, then I need proof that you are a human being and not an alien.

Ingredients:

2 tablespoons of butter

2 firmly packed tablespoons of dark brown sugar

1 tablespoon of granulated sugar

Pinch of salt

1/4 teaspoon of pure vanilla extract

1 egg yolk

1/4 teaspoon of baking soda

1/4 cup of all-purpose flour

3 heaping tablespoons of semisweet chocolate chips

Directions:

1. Start by preheating the toaster oven to 350 degrees.
2. Soften butter and combine with sugars, salt, and vanilla.
3. Add egg yolk and continue to stir.
4. Add flour and baking soda and stir until combined.
5. Add chocolate chips to the bowl and mix until evenly spread.
6. Line a pan with parchment paper and separate dough into two equal parts onto pan.
7. Bake for 8 minutes.

Nutritional Info: Calories: 667, Sodium: 645 mg, Dietary Fiber: 3.1 g, Total Fat: 39.9 g, Total Carbs: 73.4 g, Protein: 6.2 g.

Strawberry Chocolate Chip Banana Bread Bars

Servings: 10 | Prep Time: 15 Minutes | Cook Time: 30 Minutes

The name really says it all. This desert is not only relatively healthy, but it will easily become a standard in the household.

Ingredients:

1 1/4 cups white whole wheat flour

1 cup old-fashioned rolled oats

1 teaspoon ground cinnamon

1 1/2 teaspoons baking soda

2 bananas

1 egg

1/4 cup packed brown sugar

2 tablespoons melted coconut oil

3/4 cups + 1 tablespoon reduced-fat buttermilk

1 cup freeze-dried strawberries

1/4 cup semi-sweet mini chocolate chips

Directions:

1. Start by preheating the toaster oven to 350 degrees.

2. Stir dry ingredients together in a medium bowl. Mash bananas and mix with egg, then add sugar, oil, and buttermilk.

3. Combine flour mixture with banana mixture. Fold in strawberries and chocolate chips.

4. Pour batter into a greased cake pan and bake for 30 minutes. Allow to cool then return to pan.

Nutritional Info: Calories: 187, Sodium: 220 mg, Dietary Fiber: 2.4 g, Total Fat: 5.4 g, Total Carbs: 31.1 g, Protein: 4.5 g.

13

Pantry

A cook is only as good as the ingredients that they have at their disposal. When it comes to baking/broiling/roasting there are certain ingredients that you should always have filling your pantry.

FRUITS AND VEGETABLES – Having fruits and veggies on hand is important for cooking many dishes, they are also great for a snack while cooking.

BREAD – Not just your run of the mill sandwich bread either, keep some Texas toast on hand for some home-made garlic bread.

NUTS – Keep your favorite nuts on hand for roasting or cooking. Almonds, walnuts, chestnuts, and hazelnuts are just a few of the most popular nuts for roasting.

FLOUR - Flour is an important ingredient in many facets of frying. You won't be able to bake without flour.

SUGAR - Sugar is obviously an important part of sweet snacks and baked goods so you would be stuck without it if you are planning on some light baking.

DRIED HERBS - If we listed each of these individually we would be here all day. Dried herbs include oregano, parsley, rosemary, thyme, etc. They last forever and can be used to make an ordinary recipe extraordinary.

SPICES – Spices get a category all their own because they are all unique blends. All spice, chili powder, cinnamon, and curry powder are just a few spices that should always be in your pantry.

PLATES/TINS/PANS – Make sure that you stock your cabinets with plates that can withstand the heat of the toaster oven. This is an added benefit, not only because you can reheat on them, but you can also use your toaster oven to warm the plates and serve hot food on warm plates. Also be sure to stock pans and tins that are small enough to fit into the oven.

CRACKERS – You would be surprised how many toaster oven recipes call for crackers, but in this case your crackers need a toaster oven. A toaster oven can bring stale crackers back to life and make them brand new again.

CHOCOLATE – Some people may find it shocking that not everyone stocks chocolate in their pantry, but some people have not yet experienced the magic of chocolate. There is always a need for chocolate whether you are using it to bake, to make s'mores in your oven, or just to snack on while you cook.

POTATOES – There are so many ways you can cook potatoes in a toaster oven that there could almost be a cook book in itself for toaster oven potatoes. It is an important ingredient in some main dishes and especially important in side dishes that are perfect for the toaster oven.

.

Next Steps...

DID YOU ENJOY THE BOOK?

IF SO, THEN LET ME KNOW BY LEAVING A REVIEW ON AMAZON! Reviews are the lifeblood of independent authors. I would appreciate even a few words and rating if that's all you have time for. Here's the link:

http://www.healthyhappyfoodie.org/ee1-freebooks

IF YOU DID NOT LIKE THIS BOOK, THEN PLEASE TELL ME! Email me at feedback@HHFpress.com and let me know what you didn't like! Perhaps I can change it. In today's world a book doesn't have to be stagnant, it can improve with time and feedback from readers like you. You can impact this book, and I welcome your feedback. Help make this book better for everyone!

DO YOU LIKE FREE BOOKS?

Every month we release a new book, and we offer it to our current readers first...absolutely free! This helps us get early feedback before launching a book, and lets you stock your shelf full of interesting and valuable books for free!

Some recent titles include:

- The Complete Vegetable Spiralizer Cookbook
- My Lodge Cast Iron Skillet Cookbook
- 101 The New Crepes Cookbook

To receive this month's free book, just go to

http://www.healthyhappyfoodie.org/ee1-freebooks

Made in the USA
San Bernardino, CA
30 January 2019